Believe
God

A BLACK AND WHITE
CHALLENGE TO CULTURAL
RELIGIOUS BELIEFS

FP SCHWARZ

ISBN: 979-8-9929443-0-3

Copyright © 2025 by FP Schwarz

Scripture taken from the HOLY BIBLE, NEW INTERNATIONAL VERSION. Copyright 1973, 1978, 1984 International Bible Society. Used by permission of Zondervan Bible Publishers.

This book also contains an original paraphrase of the Gospel of John in its entirety. This paraphrase is based on the King James Version of the Bible and is not a direct translation of the original biblical manuscripts. Instead, it is a rewriting of the King James text into modern, conversational English.

Book Cover Design by ebooklaunch.com

Truth is like a lion.
You don't have to defend it.

Let it loose… it will defend itself.
Augustine of Hippo

PREFACE

We often treat belief and truth as if they are the same thing. They are not.

A belief is something we choose to believe.

Truth is something we discover to be true.

Beliefs come from many places—family, culture, pain, hope, disappointment, and desire. They develop over the course of a lifetime as we accumulate experiences, engage in discussions, consume media, and process information—then blend it all with our feelings and emotions, and this shapes the way we interpret the world around us. As our individual beliefs accumulate, they form an overarching belief system. But this process does not ensure that these beliefs reflect objective truth.

Truth exists independent of belief.

It is not shaped by our feelings, our backgrounds, or our preferences.

If something is true, it remains true whether we accept it, reject it, or ignore it.

And if something is false, believing it passionately doesn't make it real.

Our perception may evolve, but reality itself doesn't move.

We can rename, reinterpret, or recast a thing in a different light—but none of that has the power to change what is objectively real. Truth stands firm, even when we're unsure of it.

Knowledge begins when we are willing to ask what is true.

Wisdom begins when we allow the answer to shape how we live.

Finding truth is like uncovering a lost treasure—the sacrifices made in pursuit of a treasure, pale in comparison to the value of the discovery.

The purpose of this book is simple: to invite you to look at faith in Christ not as a religious experience, but as an encounter with truth itself.

Not tradition, not culture, not emotion—truth.

This book is not written to persuade, defend, or argue.

It is written to challenge the reader to consider that faith is not a system of rituals or beliefs we embrace, but a personal response to what is real, eternal, and unchanging.

Because in the end, it doesn't matter what you happen to believe.

What matters is whether what you believe is actually true.

WHAT IS TRUTH?

The twentieth century stands out as one of the most transformative eras in recorded history. Before its arrival, cultural change moved at a glacial pace that was mostly imperceptible across generations.

The twenty-first century arrived in an atmosphere of great expectation and hope, and cultural change accelerated with increased knowledge and dependence on technology. The degree of change in the cultural experience between a grandparent and grandchild today is far greater than ten generations had to accommodate before the 1900s. This raises a pressing question: How much more transformation will society undergo in the next hundred years, especially with the rapid advancements in artificial intelligence?

Technology often lures us into believing in the inherent superiority of modern culture over past generations. Modern society is producing future generations of self-confident, self-sufficient, and self-improving people. We are independent, free-thinking, and confident in our understanding of truth, and generally complacent in our thoughts of God. We live in a generation that holds religion, like superstition, to be rooted in individual wisdom—beauty is in the eye of the beholder and truth is in the mind of the thinker. This relativistic outlook profoundly influences the cultural understanding of life, death, and God.

Relativism is the subtle philosophy in our culture that denies the existence of absolute truth and reduces facts to the level of opinions. It dulls the fear of death by allowing us to create our own spiritual reality by pronouncing personal beliefs as truth. But like a man who walks with the confidence and security of past experience across a frozen lake, we must evaluate our foundational beliefs to confirm that these beliefs are actually true. Like thawing ice, relativism has been very subtle in eroding the foundation of truth in our culture.

Consider these illustrations of how relativism has shaped our perceptions of what is true:

> I've been doing a lot of thinking on the subject of gravity. I have examined the research and discussed what I believe with others, and I am convinced that I am right. I believe I can take a running jump off a 300-foot cliff, and if I hold out my arms and feet in just the right way, I will float gently to the ground. I feel this is right! I believe this is what the scientists are saying about the law of gravity, and I know I can safely jump off a 300-foot cliff without anything but my Nikes to cushion the fall. I took science classes as a kid, and I am willing to stake my life on what I believe. I have listened to the arrogant hypocrites who believe that if someone were to jump off a cliff, they would be crushed by the fall. But they have no right to condemn me. They claim to have substance to their theory, but I believe I do too, and we should just accept each other as we are. I haven't taken the jump yet,

*and like most, I am a little afraid of it. But I know what
I believe, and it works for me!*

After reading such a statement, most recognize the absurdity of truth being relative to individual beliefs. But look at what happens when relativism is applied to spiritual truth:

*I've been doing a lot of thinking on the subject of God.
I have examined the different beliefs, and I have discussed what I believe with others, and I am convinced
that I am right. I believe that if I am a genuinely good
person and I believe in God and in the goodness of the
universe—I will go to heaven when I die. I believe this
is what the Bible says and what preachers and social
media influencers say about a God of love and how
Jesus died for my sin. I know that if I live my truth, the
universe will do right by me. I went to church as a kid,
and I am willing to stake my eternal destiny on what
I believe. I have listened to the arrogant hypocrites who
believe that they know the true way to God, but they have
no right to condemn me. They claim to have substance to
what they believe, but I feel that I do too, and we should
just accept each other as we are. I'll admit that I am a
little nervous about dying, but who isn't? I know what I
believe, and it works for me!*

Most would agree that the first statement is foolish, but the second statement seems reasonable. The first statement contradicts what our experience tells us is true about the law of gravity, while the second statement reflects a commonly held belief in our culture, so we do not notice a contradiction. But for one who has experienced the Truth of God, both statements are equally absurd.

WHAT IS THE BIBLE?

Modern religions, philosophies, and belief systems, all acknowledge a Higher Power or connection with The Universe. The Bible has gradually grown out of fashion in recent years, but it remains a must read for the understanding of spiritual truth. To experience the truth of God is to know personally what the Bible says about God and about mankind. It is more than just an intellectual acknowledgment of God; it is an experience that involves the mind, the emotions, and the spirit. It is when the spiritual dimension of our being is awakened that there is a knowledge and experience of God beyond what can be fully comprehended solely on the intellectual level. This experience is the essence of faith. It starts when we hear from God—not an audible hearing, but a hearing evidenced by a longing in our heart to know God. Romans 10:17 says, **"Faith comes from hearing the message, and the message is heard through the word of God."** It is an experience that results from hearing and believing God's word to us—hearing the words and receiving the message of the Bible.

The Bible is called the inspired Word of God. It is as if God penned every word Himself so that we could know the truth about His character. It was written by over forty different human authors in a fifteen-hundred-year time span over three continents (Africa, Asia, and Europe), and in three different languages (Hebrew, Aramaic, and Greek). Yet, it does not reflect the disharmony one would expect from such diverse origins. Josh McDowell illustrated the extraordinary history of the Bible when he wrote:

> Lest anyone think this isn't something marvelous, we'd like to give you this challenge. Find ten people from your local area who have similar educational backgrounds, all speak the same language, and all are from basically the same culture, then separate them and ask them to write their opinion on only one controversial subject, such as the meaning of life.

> When they have finished, compare the conclusions of these ten writers. Do they agree with each other? Of course not. But the Bible did not consist of merely ten authors, but 40. It was not written in one generation, but over a period of 1,500 years; not by authors with the same education, culture and language, but with vastly different education, many different cultures, from three different languages, and finally not just one subject but hundreds.

> And yet the Bible is a unity. There is complete harmony, which cannot be explained by coincidence or collusion. The unity of the Bible is a strong argument in

favor of its divine inspiration.

The unity of the Scriptures is only one reason among many which supports the Bible's claim to be the divine Word of God. Others which could be explained in detail are the testimony of the early Church, the witness of history and archaeology, and the evidence of changed lives throughout the centuries, to name but a few.[1]

Religious wars, cult leaders, dishonest "tele-evangelists," and religious hypocrites do more to discredit the Christian faith than do the most vocal and educated skeptics of the Bible. When we put aside all the opinions about God and look to the Bible as the authoritative Word of God, we can learn who God is and what life is all about.

Mark Twain said, *"It is not the things I don't understand in the Bible that bother me. It's the things I do understand."* One of the things we can understand from the Bible is that man is a spiritual being created in the image of God and for fellowship with God. The Bible confirms what most people know intrinsically—there is more to us than the flesh and bones in which our being resides. As the womb is a place where we develop and grow before being born into reality, in a similar way, this life is a prelude to an eternal reality. Knowing the truth about who God is, gives us a purpose in this life and a vision for eternity. Mark Twain is not the only one who gets uncomfortable contemplating that this world is just the preamble to an eternal reality.

The judgment of God is not a pleasant topic. But the grace of God more than makes up for the unpleasantness. Truth is inescapable; the truth will always prevail, regardless of what we believe. Some say that the God of love, as described in the New Testament, is not the God of judgment described in the Old Testament. Such a statement exposes a shallow knowledge of God. This is like seeing only the hand of a man and saying they know what the whole man looks like.

A faith that honors God is a faith that not only believes *in* God, but a faith that also *believes God*; it believes what God says and believes what the Bible says whether we like it or not. It is not enough to believe in God or in a higher power. We owe it to ourselves to discover what God says. Only then can we determine if what the what Bible says is actually true. This discovery transforms faith from "I believe in God" to "I believe God."

WHAT IS RELIGION AND
SPIRITUALITY?

R eligion plays a key, though sometimes subtle, role in our culture. Every year, statistics show that an overwhelming majority of the population believe in God. The faith of the first generations of Americans inspired "In God We Trust" on our currency and "One Nation Under God" in our pledge of allegiance. But today, we find America in a post-Christian culture and the Judeo-Christian values held by the Founding Fathers are being replaced with a humanistic and secular morality. People still believe in God, spirituality, and the supernatural, but they give very little consideration to what they believe or why they believe it. It's part of our culture to be a Christian, but the culture no longer makes it clear what a Christian is. It's part of our culture to be spiritually minded, but the truth of a matter is not considered a requirement for spiritual ideas.

Is being a Christian the same as being a good American? Good Americans are those who help their fellow man. They are honest and hardworking, somewhat religious, and lead a "good life." When such a good American dies, is there ever a doubt that he is in heaven? The conventional wisdom of our culture assures us that heaven is filled with such "good" people. The Bible is an important source of spiritual truth; how does conventional wisdom compare with the teaching of the Bible?

The theology of the culture preaches tolerance of all viewpoints. It has as its goal and its substance things such as comfort, pleasure, and good works. Cultural theology denies or trivializes the things we don't want to believe, and it changes with each new generation. The culture regards the Bible as inconceivable or obsolete. It holds no reverence for God but looks to those of celebrity status for inspiration.

To put these cultural ideas into perspective, consider the times. These times in which we live are like no other in human history. Alvin Toffler illustrated this when he wrote:

> It has been pointed out for example, that in 6000 B.C. the fastest transportation available to man over long distances was the camel caravan, averaging eight miles per hour. It was not until about 1600 B.C. [4,400 years later] when the chariot was invented that the maximum speed was raised to roughly twenty miles per hour.

> So impressive was this invention, so difficult was it to exceed this speed limit, that nearly 3,500 years later, when the first mail coach began operating in England in 1784, it averaged a mere ten mph. The first steam locomotive, introduced in 1825, could muster a top speed of only thirteen mph, and the great sailing ships of that time labored along at less than half that speed. It was probably not until the 1880's that man, with the help of

a more advanced steam locomotive, managed to reach a speed of one hundred mph. It took the human race millions of years to attain that record.

It took only fifty-eight years, however, to quadruple the limit, so that by 1938 airborne man was cracking the 400-mph line. It took a mere twenty-year flick of time to double the limit again. And by the 1960's rocket planes approached speeds of 4000 mph, and men in space capsules were circling the earth at 18,000 mph. Plotted on a graph, the line representing progress in the past generation would leap vertically off the page.

Whether we examine distances traveled, altitudes reached, minerals mined, or explosive power harnessed, the same accelerative trend is obvious. The pattern, here and in a thousand other statistical series, is absolutely clear and unmistakable. Millennia or centuries go by, and then, in our own time, a sudden bursting of the limits, a fantastic spurt forward.[1]

It is no wonder why the culture no longer has a respect for God. God created the universe, but what man has achieved in this generation is also pretty impressive. Toffler wrote this in 1970, and today we can add countless examples of remarkable change and expanded understanding. Our conception of God may be changing in these accelerated times, but our increased knowledge and accomplishment do not mean God has changed.

Fifty years ago, when a high school girl got pregnant, it was a tragedy. Today, schools hand out condoms and provide abortion services. The problems in schools are no longer talking in class, gum chewing, and smoking in the bathroom. They are guns, violence, drugs, and sexually transmitted diseases. We will imprison a person for disturbing the egg of a spotted owl, but we will allow abortions on demand in the name of choice. The boundaries of right and wrong, good and bad, and true and false are so blurred in our culture that our understanding of God is also blurred.

The Bible once defined the standard of right and wrong in our society, but now it holds no meaningful influence to most of those who own one. Consider the attitude of our culture as expressed by contemporary movies, music, and politics. Much of what we hear in the news and see in our communities is evidence of the spiritual decay of our times. The sixties' generation noticed this and proclaimed, "God is dead." But a more accurate description of our times is found in Romans 1:28. **"Since they did not think it worthwhile to retain the knowledge of God, he gave them over to a depraved mind, to do what ought not to be done."** The culture has disregarded the **"knowledge of God."** Ignorance is now commonplace—ignorance of God and ignorance of what the Bible is and ignorance of what the Bible says.

The Christian religion is often confused with the Christian faith. Religion demands duty, while faith is out of devotion. Religion condemns failure, while faith is comforted in the mercy and grace of God. Religion ignores and denies what cannot be understood, while faith believes and hopes and perseveres in truth. Religion disappoints, while faith offers the only lasting fulfillment that can be found in this life. The source of religion is man, while the source of faith is God. Religion can be seen by man and in man, but faith sees God.

It is not by religion that we can know God—it is by faith. Faith goes deeper than believing; it is knowing and experiencing that God is. Faith sees God and knows that heaven alone can fulfill the desires of the heart. Faith rejoices and hurts, comforts and disturbs, works and rests, all of the time and at the same time. No religious experience can produce such a paradoxical life, only an encounter with the living God of the Bible. The message of the cross of Jesus Christ is that man can truly know God and not just know about God. Jesus said, **"Here I am! I stand at the door and knock. If anyone hears my voice and opens the door, I will come in and eat with him and he with me"** **(Revelation 3:20).**

To those who answer this call, this life is the closest thing to hell they will ever experience. To those who reject the truth, this life may be the closest thing to heaven they will ever experience. For heaven and hell are very real, and this life and this time is the only separation between these two eternal destinies.

2 Corinthians 13:5 gives us this challenge: **"Examine yourselves to see whether you are in the faith; test yourselves. Do you not realize that Christ Jesus is in you—unless, of course, you fail the test?"** To be **"in the faith"** means that **"Christ Jesus is in you."** To be a Christian means that the same Jesus whose life, death, and resurrection is celebrated around the world, lives and dwells in your physical being. This is the Christian experience! The New Testament book of Romans describes this dichotomy of being:

> **You, however, are controlled not by the sinful nature but by the Spirit, if the Spirit of God lives in you. And if anyone does not have the Spirit of Christ, he does not belong to Christ. But if Christ is in you, your body is dead to sin, yet your**

**spirit is alive because of righteousness. And if the
Spirit of him who raised Jesus from the dead is
living in you, he who raised Christ from the dead
will also give life to your mortal bodies through
his Spirit, who lives in you. (Romans 8:9–11)**

A Christian is one who possess the Spirit of God. One who has answered God's call and is born again. **"If anyone is in Christ, he is a new creation; the old has gone, the new has come" (2 Corinthians 5:17).** Being born again is like a man who has been physically blind all his life. Then, one day he wakes up and miraculously he can see. All those things he thought he understood now make more sense. All the things he could not understand such as color, beauty, and light are now a part of his everyday experience. Just as a blind man who can now see is drastically changed from what he was, so is the person who is spiritually born again. All those things he thought he understood now make more sense. All the things he could not understand about life and death, good and evil, are now real everyday experiences.

WHAT IS BORN AGAIN?

The term "born again" was first spoken by Jesus to one of the religious leaders of His day. To better understand this term, let's look at the context in which Jesus used it.

Now there was a man of the Pharisees named Nicodemus, a member of the Jewish ruling council. He came to Jesus at night and said, "Rabbi, we know you are a teacher who has come from God. For no one could perform the miraculous signs you are doing if God were not with him."

In reply Jesus declared, "I tell you the truth, no one can see the kingdom of God unless he is born again."

"How can a man be born when he is old?" Nicodemus asked. "Surely he cannot enter a second time into his mother's womb to be born!"

Jesus answered, "I tell you the truth, no one can
enter the kingdom of God unless he is born of
water and the Spirit. Flesh gives birth to flesh,
but the Spirit gives birth to spirit. You should
not be surprised at my saying, 'You must be born
again.' The wind blows wherever it pleases. You
hear its sound, but you cannot tell where it comes
from or where it is going. So it is with everyone
born of the Spirit."

"How can this be?" Nicodemus asked. (John
3:1–9)

Nicodemus was wise enough to recognize that Jesus was sent from
God and knew that his PhD in religion was missing something very
important. So, he goes to Jesus for advice and is told that what he is
missing is spiritual life. Not life that animates the flesh, but life that
ignites the spirit. A spiritual birth that is just as real and just as dramatic
and just as miraculous as a physical birth. The beginning of a new life
when the Spirit of God comes into your physical being and you are
changed from the inside out. An experience that changes prayer from
a religious exercise to a conversation between two friends.

Nicodemus is confused. This was a strange and new idea. Two
thousand years later, it is still unfamiliar. As it is written:

And even if our gospel is veiled, it is veiled to
those who are perishing. The god of this age has
blinded the minds of unbelievers, so that they

cannot see the light of the gospel of the glory of
Christ, who is the image of God. (2 Corinthians
4:3–4)

The man without the Spirit does not accept the
things that come from the Spirit of God, for they
are foolishness to him, and he cannot understand
them, because they are spiritually discerned. (1
Corinthians 2:14)

Spiritually discerned, or spiritually separated from God and spiritually dead, is man's condition before being **"born of the Spirit."**
Nicodemus, although being a religious leader, lacked the insight into
the deeper realities of God. He had an intellectual acceptance of the
truths of God, but not the experience. Nicodemus was well versed
in the Scriptures but was drawn to Jesus because he knew that Jesus
possessed more than just knowledge. Jesus possessed the spiritual life
necessary to discern spiritual truth. This is the life Jesus gives to this
day—the life we receive when we are **"born of the Spirit."**

Jesus describes the born-again experience with this analogy: **"The
wind blows wherever it pleases. You hear its sound, but you
cannot tell where it comes from or where it is going. So it
is with everyone born of the Spirit."** The born-again experience
is surrounded by mystery. Like the wind, we do not know where it
comes from or where it will go. We cannot see it, but we see its effects.
We cannot hold it, but we can feel its presence. Being born again is
knowing God. It is seeing and hearing for the first time as if being blind
and deaf before.

Jesus explains this to Nicodemus as the conversation continues:

"How can this be?" Nicodemus asked.

"You are Israel's teacher," said Jesus, "and do you
not understand these things? I tell you the truth,
we speak of what we know, and we testify to what
we have seen, but still, you people do not accept
our testimony. I have spoken to you of earthly
things and you do not believe; how then will you
believe if I speak of heavenly things? No one has
ever gone into heaven except the one who came
from heaven—the Son of Man. Just as Moses lifted up the snake in the desert, so the Son of Man
must be lifted up, that everyone who believes in
him may have eternal life." (John 3:9–15)

These words were directed at a religious leader, and they are words
to the religious and the religiously complacent people today. Jesus says
the first problem is you don't believe our testimony; you don't believe
what we say about the things we have seen and experienced. There
are countless people around the world whose lives are a testimony of
the power and grace of an awesome God. Their humility keeps them
from being noticed, and their selflessness is often ignored. They are
not perfect, but they are real—and so is the Spirit of God that dwells in
them. They are those who look to Jesus Christ and have believed His
testimony as found in the New Testament Gospels (Matthew, Mark,
Luke, and John). They are not religious zealots but genuine followers
of Christ.

Furthermore, Jesus says, **"No one has ever gone into heaven except the one who came from heaven—the Son of Man."** Jesus is different from Mohammed, Buddha, and every other spiritual leader who has ever walked the face of the earth, because Jesus came from heaven, and heaven is our greatest need as human beings. And if we dare to believe the testimony and look to Jesus as a source of life rather than an object of religion, then we will experience a quickening in our spirit—that is the new birth.

Jesus painted a picture with words that Nicodemus would certainly understand because it is a story in the Old Testament. **"Just as Moses lifted up the snake in the desert, so the Son of Man must be lifted up, that everyone who believes in him may have eternal life."** Jesus is referring to a historical event from the time of Moses when the Israelites were wandering through the desert. It was after God released them from a life of slavery in Egypt but before they entered the land that God had promised them.

> **They traveled from Mount Hor along the route to the Red Sea, to go around Edom. But the people grew impatient on the way; they spoke against God and against Moses, and said, "Why have you brought us up out of Egypt to die in the desert? There is no bread! There is no water! And we detest this miserable food!"**
>
> **Then the Lord sent venomous snakes among them; they bit the people and many Israelites died. The people came to Moses and said, "We sinned when we spoke against the Lord and against you. Pray that the Lord will take the**

snakes away from us." So Moses prayed for the people.

The Lord said to Moses, "Make a snake and put it up on a pole; anyone who is bitten can look at it and live." So Moses made a bronze snake and put it up on a pole. Then when anyone was bitten by a snake and looked at the bronze snake, he lived. (Numbers 21:4–9)

The people grumbled against God because they didn't like their circumstances. Their grumbling invoked God's judgment and brought death. Those bitten by the snakes knew they would die, and they cried out to God for help. God could have answered their prayer by just speaking a word. By a word from God, the snakes would have disappeared, and the people would have been healed. But that was not how God chose to do it. God provided a way to escape the death that they brought upon themselves, but the way God provided required something unconventional—the provision required faith. God gave them a choice: **"when anyone was bitten by a snake and looked at the bronze snake, he lived."** If they would step out in an act of faith, and believe the message God spoke through Moses, then they would live. If they didn't take that step of faith, they would face the consequences of that decision. It may not have made much sense at the time, but it was what God provided, and it was what God required.

Jesus Christ was lifted up on a cross for the whole world and for every generation to look at to receive God's salvation. **"Just as Moses lifted up the snake in the desert, so the Son of Man must be lifted up, that everyone who believes in him may have eternal life."** Ezekiel 18:20 tells us **"The soul who sins is the one who will** die." And in Romans 6:23 we are told, **"For the wages of sin is death, but the gift of God is eternal life in Jesus Christ our Lord."** Like venomous snakes, sin dwells among us and condemns us to death. But if we step out in faith and look to Jesus, we will not receive the sting of death, but the **"gift of God is eternal life."** Physical life is the essence of being born in the flesh; eternal life is the essence of being born of the Spirit. It may not make much sense, but it is what God has provided, and it is what God requires.

As the conversation with Nicodemus continues, Jesus describes how and why the born-again experience is necessary. Jesus explains his declaration that **"no one can see the kingdom of God unless he is born again" (John 3:3).**

> **"For God so loved the world that he gave his one and only Son, that whoever believes in him shall not perish but have eternal life. For God did not send his Son into the world to condemn the world, but to save the world through him. Whoever believes in him is not condemned, but whoever does not believe stands condemned already because he has not believed in the name of God's one and only Son." (John 3:16–18)**

Without spiritual birth, we are without spiritual life. Without spiritual life we **"stand condemned already."** Those are strong and terrifying words. But those words are why Jesus came from heaven to rescue those who **"stand condemned already."** We stand condemned not because of something we did, but because of what we are—sinners. God saw the "condemned" state of mankind and chose to do something about it. **"For God so loved the world that he gave his one and only Son, that whoever believes in him shall not perish but have eternal life."** Out of love and compassion, God sent a cure to give life to our dead souls.

Jesus alluded to the Old Testament story of Moses and the bronze snake to illustrate a people in need of a miracle. The people had been bitten by snakes and were about to die. When faced with death, their perspective on things changed quickly from an attitude of complaining to one of repentance. When Jesus says, **"whoever does not believe stands condemned already,"** this phrase should be like a snake bite to us. Just as those bitten by snakes were condemned to a physical death, those who do not believe are condemned to a spiritual death.

The alternative to standing condemned is to believe in God's one and only Son: **"that whoever believes in him shall not perish but have eternal life."** To believe in Jesus is to believe that He is the Son of God who lived a perfect and sinless life on this earth and was condemned to die. He rose from the dead and lives today in the hearts of people who have received Him. In receiving Him, we receive the righteous life the He lived. The sinful life that we live, in essence, died on the cross two thousand years ago. This truth is summarized in Romans 3:22–24 (emphasis added): **"This righteousness from God comes through faith in Jesus Christ to all who believe. There is no difference, for <u>all have sinned and fall short of the glory of God,</u>** (*the snake bite*) **and are justified freely by his grace through the redemption that came by <u>Christ Jesus</u>"** (*The bronze snake God provides to survive the snake bite*).

We are not told, but we could speculate that some who were bitten by the snakes in the desert may have thought that Moses's bronze snake solution was bizarre. Others may have rejected the idea, thinking there must be a more logical or scientific way. Still others may have thought that they had not been bitten too badly and did not need to look at the bronze snake. Some may have even liked the snakes and didn't believe they were really poisonous. These are the beliefs that Jesus addresses in the conclusion of his conversation with Nicodemus:

This is the verdict: Light has come into the world, but men loved darkness instead of light because their deeds were evil. Everyone who does evil hates the light and will not come into the light for fear that his deeds will be exposed. But whoever lives by the truth comes into the light, so that it may be seen plainly that what he has done has been done through God." (John 3:19–21)

Truth is something that must simply be accepted. Something that is true remains true whether we believe it or not. Something that is true remains true whether we know about it or not. The real question is not "What do you believe?" but simply "Do you believe?" Do you believe that the words Jesus spoke to Nicodemus are true? Do you believe the Bible is really the inspired Word of God?

Consider the words Jesus spoke at the end of His discussion with Nicodemus: **"Light has come into the world, but men loved darkness instead of light because their deeds were evil. Everyone who does evil hates the light and will not come into the light for fear that his deeds will be exposed."** We must all decide if the Bible is true. Is the Bible a light that exposes sin? Does sin really result in death and eternal darkness?

In this age of positive thinking and healthy self-esteem, we have been trained to ignore and deny negative thoughts about ourselves.

But if we receive the truth about ourselves as revealed in the Bible that we are **"dead in our transgressions and sins" (Ephesians 2:1)** and accept the gift of God, which is life in Jesus Christ, then we can experience life as God intended it to be.

The truth is laid out for us, but it is nothing but words unless it is received as the truth. Today, as in every generation, we are confronted with the choice to accept or reject Jesus's words as truth. The people of Jesus's day discussed this very issue. They were wondering what Jesus was going to do during a national holiday celebration, and from this event we can see how Jesus addressed this skepticism:

> **Now at the Feast, the Jews were watching for him and asking, "Where is that man?"**
>
> **Among the crowds there was widespread whispering about him. Some said, "He is a good man."**
>
> **Others replied, "No, he deceives the people." But no one would say anything publicly about him for fear of the Jews.**
>
> **Not until halfway through the Feast did Jesus go up to the temple courts and begin to teach. The Jews were amazed and asked, "How did this man get such learning without having studied?"**
>
> **Jesus answered, "My teaching is not my own. It comes from him who sent me. If anyone chooses to do God's will, he will find out whether my**

**teaching comes from God or whether I speak on
my own." (John 7:11–17)**

Beliefs come in all shapes and sizes. Different cultures, different upbringings, different "holy books" represent different beliefs. Jesus says, **"My teaching is not my own. It comes from him who sent me. If anyone chooses to do God's will, he will find out whether my teaching comes from God or whether I speak on my own."** The truth is a treasure to be discovered. Jesus is The Way, The Truth, and The Life. The way to discover the truth is to choose **"to do God's will"** and believe God. Or we can ignore truth and choose to believe in religion, prophets, holy books, philosophies, and a variety of teachers and teachings.

We *choose* what we believe, but we *discover* what is true.

WHAT IS FAITH VERSUS RELIGION?

To be born again of the Spirit is to believe God's Word, receive God's Spirit, and choose to do God's will. It is a change in attitude and in outlook about the meaning of life. It is discerning sin and righteousness as we discern night and day. It is *not* about becoming religious but about discovering the reality of God.

Jesus told a story about two men, one a sinner and one a very religious man. This story illustrates the difference between those who trust in themselves and those who believe God at His word:

> **To some who were confident of their own righteousness and looked down on everybody else, Jesus told this parable:**
>
> **"Two men went up to the temple to pray, one a Pharisee and the other a tax collector. The Pharisee stood up and prayed about himself: 'God, I**

thank you that I am not like other men—robbers, evildoers, adulterers—or even like this tax collector. I fast twice a week and give a tenth of all I get.'

"But the tax collector stood at a distance. He would not even look up to heaven, but beat his breast and said, 'God, have mercy on me, a sinner.'

"I tell you the truth, this man rather than the other went home justified before God. For everyone who exalts himself will be humbled, and he who humbles himself will be exalted." (Luke 18:9–14)

A religious person could read this story and say with all sincerity, *"Thank You, Lord, that I am not like that Pharisee."* But one who has discovered the reality of God cries out like the tax collector, **"God, have mercy on me, a sinner."** Being born again of the Spirit is not something we do, but something that God does in us—something that happens to us when God reveals Himself to us. Just as Jesus summed up in His conversation with Nicodemus: **"But whoever lives by the truth comes into the light, so that it may be seen plainly that what he has done has been done through God"** **(John 3:21).** Being born again is seeing God by believing His Word. It is a change in one's life that results not from a decision to be a better person, but a decision to believe God. A decision that results in being astonished, amazed, and humbled before God—an experience that simply believing in God could never produce.

We are faced with the question that either God created man or man created God; either man was created in God's image as described in the Bible, or man created God in man's image. To believe in God without believing God's Word is the same thing as creating God in your own image. But to believe God is to believe His Word to us, and in believing we are changed. For some, the change is dramatic and quick; for others, it is subtle over time. But no one can remain unchanged who passes from death to life and becomes a dwelling place of the Spirit of God.

Hear the challenge of 2 Corinthians 13:5: **"Examine yourselves to see whether you are in the faith; test yourselves. Do you not realize that Christ Jesus is in you—unless, of course, you fail the test?"** It is not an issue of religious preference but a choice with eternal significance. A choice to receive God's provision by believing and receiving His Word or rejecting the truth in exchange for the culturally inspired beliefs about eternity and heaven.

Examine your beliefs about God and heaven. Discover, what the Bible says about sin and holiness before settling for religious clichés. Only then are you prepared and informed to know if the Christian faith is a manmade attempt to reach out to God, or if the Bible is God's inspired word to reach out to you. Take the time to hear what God has to say. Eternity is a very long time to rejoice or weep over your answer to the question "Who is God?"

BELIEVE GOD

The remainder of this book is an original paraphrase of the Gospel of John, based on the King James Version of the Bible. This paraphrase is not a direct translation of the original biblical manuscripts. Instead, it is a modern, conversational rewriting of the King James text.

The Gospel of John was written by the Apostle John, one of the original twelve disciples of Jesus. John is often referred to as "John the Beloved" because of his deep love for Jesus and the special love Jesus had for him in return.

This paraphrased version omits the verse numbers found in traditional Bible translations, allowing the text to flow more naturally, similar to how John originally wrote it. However, chapter numbers are included for easy reference to standard Bible translations.

The Gospel of John is part of the New Testament, but it is also a firsthand account of who Jesus is from one of His closest disciples. John's Gospel differs from the other three books that describe the life of Christ—Matthew, Mark, and Luke—because it is more than just a historical record of Jesus' life. Instead, it highlights the divinity and spiritual significance of His existence. As John reveals who Jesus is, Jesus, in turn, reveals who God is.

As you read the Gospel of John, don't think of it as reading the Bible in a traditional sense—approach it as reading the testimony of someone who was there, sharing a firsthand account of who Jesus is. Keep an open mind and consider that John was a real person who truly believed everything he wrote. Then the question becomes: ***Do you believe that what John says is, in fact, true?***

Most of the religious leaders of Jesus' day did not believe what He said. Jesus did not conform to their religious traditions or their preconceived ideas about God. If you are skeptical or critical of religion and religious institutions, you may find that you have more in common with Jesus—*and with John*—than you think.

John does not present the Christian faith as a religion; rather, he describes a people born again of the Spirit, alive in Christ, because of the reality of God. He explains how Jesus came from heaven, not to establish a religion, but to enable us to know God personally. The children of God are not merely a "New Testament religious community"; they are those who love God and love others, recognizing that all people are made in the image of God.

John portrays Jesus as *The Way, The Truth, and The Life*—not as *The Religion, The Rules, and The Rituals.* Jesus is the incarnation of God and the embodiment of humanity. Through John's testimony, we learn what it truly means to **Believe God**—not just to be someone who casually believes in God.

Truth is something to be discovered. Read the Gospel of John as if you were on a treasure hunt, searching for the true nature of God. Set aside your preconceived notions about religion, Christianity, or the age-old philosophical questions about the meaning of life. When you finish, ask yourself, **"What if what John says is actually true?"** Then, you have the rest of your life to think about it.

THE GOSPEL OF JOHN

JOHN CHAPTER 1

In the beginning, there was the Word. The Word was with God, and the Word was God. From the very beginning, the Word was united with God.

Everything was created through Him. Absolutely nothing came into existence without Him. In Him was life itself, and that life became the light for all people. This light shines in the darkness, and no amount of darkness could overcome it.

There was a man sent by God named John. His purpose was clear: to tell everyone about this Light so that they might believe through his testimony. Now, John wasn't the Light itself, but he was sent to point people toward the true Light. The Light that gives light to everyone, He was coming into the world.

This Light was in the world, the same world that was made through Him, yet the world did not recognize Him. He came to His own people, but His own people did not accept Him. But to anyone who did receive Him, He gave them the power to become children of God—those who believe in His name.

These people weren't born into God's family through human efforts, plans, or desires—they were born of God Himself.

And the Word became flesh. He lived among us, and we saw His glory—the glory of the one and only Son of God, full of grace and truth, sent from the Father. John testified about Him, shouting, "This is the one I was talking about! He's the one who comes after me, yet He is positioned much higher than me, because He was before me."

Out of His abundance, we have all received grace and blessing. The law was given through Moses, but grace and truth came through Jesus Christ. No one has ever seen God, but the one and only Son, who is Himself God and is closest to the Father's heart, He has made God known.

This is how John's testimony unfolded: when religious leaders from Jerusalem sent priests and Levites to ask him, "Who are you?" John didn't hold back. He made it clear, "I am not the Christ."

They pressed him, "Then who are you? Are you Elijah?"

"No, I am not," he replied.

"Are you the Prophet?"

"No."

Finally, they said, "Who are you? We need an answer to take back to those who sent us. What do you say about yourself?"

John replied, "I am the voice of someone shouting in the wilderness: 'Pepare the way for the Lord!' just as the prophet Isaiah said."

Now, some Pharisees in the group asked him, "If you're not the Christ, Elijah, or the Prophet, why are you baptizing people?"

John answered, "I baptize with water, but there is someone standing among you whom you do not recognize. He is the one coming after me, and I am not worthy to untie His sandal straps."

This all happened in Bethany, on the other side of the Jordan River, where John was baptizing people.

The next day, John saw Jesus coming toward him. He declared, "Look! The Lamb of God who takes away the sin of the world! This is the one I was telling you about—'After me comes a man who is greater than I, because He was before me.' Even I did not recognize Him at first, but I came baptizing with water so He could be revealed to Israel."

John testified, "I saw the Spirit come down from heaven like a dove and rest on Him. I did not know it was Him at first, but God, who sent me to baptize told me, 'The one you see the Spirit come down on and remain is the one who will baptize with the Holy Spirit.' I saw this happen, and I am telling you—this is the Son of God."

The next day, John was with two of his disciples when he saw Jesus walking by. He said, "Look! The Lamb of God!" Hearing this, the two disciples followed Jesus.

Jesus turned and saw them following. "What are you looking for?" He asked.

They said, "Rabbi (which means Teacher), where are you staying?"

"Come and see," Jesus replied. So, they went and spent the day with Him. It was about four in the afternoon.

One of John's disciples, Andrew, Simon Peter's brother, couldn't keep the news to himself. He found his brother Simon and said, "We have found the Messiah!" (which means Christ).

He brought Simon to Jesus, who looked at him and said, "You are Simon, son of John. From now on, you will be called Cephas" (which means Peter, or a rock).

The next day, Jesus decided to go to Galilee. He found Philip and said, "Follow Me." Philip, who was from the same town as Andrew and Peter, found Nathanael and said, "We've found the one Moses and the prophets wrote about—Jesus of Nazareth, the son of Joseph!"

Nathanael was skeptical. "Nazareth? Can anything good come from Nazareth?"

"Come and see," Philip replied.

When Jesus saw Nathanael approaching, He said, "Here is a true Israelite, a man of great integrity!"

"How do You know me?" Nathanael asked.

Jesus answered, "I saw you under the fig tree before Philip called you."

Amazed, Nathanael exclaimed, "Rabbi, You are the Son of God! You are the King of Israel!"

Jesus smiled and said, "You believe because I told you I saw you under the fig tree? You are going to see even greater things than that! Truly, I say to you, you will see heaven open and the angels of God ascending and descending upon the Son of Man."

JOHN CHAPTER 2

T hree days later, there was a wedding celebration in Cana, a town in Galilee. Jesus's mother was there, and Jesus and His disciples were also invited to the celebration.

During the feast, the wine ran out, and Jesus's mother came to Him and said, "They have no more wine."

Jesus replied, "Dear woman, why are you involving Me in this? My time has not yet come."

But His mother didn't argue. She simply told the servants, "Do whatever He tells you to do."

Nearby, there were six large stone jars used by the Jewish people for ceremonial washing. Each jar could hold 20 to 30 gallons. Jesus told the servants, "Fill the jars with water." So, they filled them to the brim. Then He said, "Now draw some out and take it to the master of the banquet." And they did.

When the master of the banquet tasted the water that had been turned into wine (though he didn't know where it had come from—the servants knew!), he called the bridegroom over and said, "Everyone serves the best wine first, and after the guests have had plenty to drink, then they bring out the cheaper wine. But you've saved the best wine for now!"

This was the first miraculous sign Jesus performed in Cana of Galilee. By this, Jesus revealed His glory, and His disciples believed in Him.

After the wedding, Jesus, His mother, His brothers, and His disciples went down to Capernaum for a short stay.

As the time for the Jewish Passover approached, Jesus traveled to Jerusalem. When He entered the temple courts, He found people selling cattle, sheep, and doves. Others were sitting at tables exchanging money. Seeing this, Jesus made a whip out of cords and drove everyone out—both the merchants and the animals. He scattered the money and overturned the tables. To those selling doves, He said, "Get these things out of here! Stop turning My Father's house into a marketplace!"

His disciples remembered the scripture that says, *"Zeal for Your house will consume me."*

Some of the Jewish leaders demanded, "What sign can You show us to prove You have the authority to do this?"

Jesus answered, "Destroy this temple, and I will raise it up in three days."

They replied, "It's taken forty-six years to build this temple, and You will to raise it up in three days?" But Jesus wasn't talking about the physical temple—He was referring to His body. After Jesus's resurrection from the dead, His disciples remembered what He had said, and they believed the scripture and His words.

While Jesus was in Jerusalem during the Passover festival, many people saw the miraculous signs He performed and believed in His name. But Jesus did not fully entrust Himself to them, because He knew all people. He did not need anyone to tell Him about humanity—He already understood what was in each person's heart.

JOHN CHAPTER 3

There was a man named Nicodemus, a Pharisee and an important leader among the Jewish people. One night, he came to Jesus and said, "Rabbi, we know you are a teacher who has come from God. No one could perform the miracles you are doing unless God was with him."

Jesus replied, "I am telling you the truth: unless someone is born again, they cannot see the kingdom of God."

Confused, Nicodemus asked, "How can someone be born when they're old? Surely, they can't go back into their mother's womb and be born again!"

Jesus explained, "I am telling you the truth: no one can enter the kingdom of God unless they are born of water and the Spirit. Human life gives birth to human life, but the Spirit gives birth to spiritual life. Do not be surprised that I said you must be born again. The wind blows wherever it wants—you hear it, but you can't see where it's coming from or where it's going. That's how it is for everyone born of the Spirit."

Still puzzled, Nicodemus asked, "How can this be?"

Jesus responded, "You are a teacher of Israel, and you don't understand these things? Listen carefully: we speak about what we know and testify to what we have seen, but you still do not accept what we're saying. If I have told you about earthly things and you don't believe it, how will you believe if I tell you about heavenly things? No one has gone up to heaven except the One who came down from heaven—the Son of Man. Just as Moses lifted up the bronze serpent in the wilderness, so the Son of Man must be lifted up, so that everyone who believes in Him may have eternal life.

"For God loved the world so much that He gave His one and only Son, so that whoever believes in Him will not perish but have eternal life. God did not send His Son into the world to condemn the world, but to save the world through Him. Whoever believes in the Son of God is not condemned, but whoever does not believe stands condemned already because they have not believed in the name of God's one and only Son.

"This is the verdict: Light has come into the world, but people loved darkness instead of the light because their actions were evil. Everyone who does evil hates the light and won't come into the light, fearing that their deeds will be exposed. But those who live by the truth come into the light, so it is clear that their actions, are done in and through God."

After this, Jesus and His disciples went into the countryside of Judea, where He spent time with them and baptized people. John was also baptizing in Aenon near Salim because there was plenty of water there, and people were coming to be baptized. (This was before John was put in prison.)

An argument about ceremonial washing started between some of John's disciples and a religious person. They came to

John and said, "Rabbi, the man you testified about, the one who was with you on the other side of the Jordan—He is baptizing, and everyone is going to Him!"

John answered, "A person can only receive what is given to them from heaven. You yourselves heard me say, 'I am not the Messiah, but I was sent ahead of Him.' The bride belongs to the bridegroom, but the friend of the bridegroom, who stands and listens, is full of joy when he hears the bridegroom's voice. That joy is mine, and it is now complete. He must become greater, and I must become less.

"The One who comes from above is above all. The one who is from the earth belongs to the earth and speaks as one from the earth. But the One who comes from heaven is above all. He speaks of what He has seen and heard, but no one accepts His testimony. Whoever does accept it confirms that God is truthful. The One that God sent speaks God's words, for God gives the Spirit without limit. The Father loves the Son and has placed everything in His hands. Whoever believes in the Son has eternal life. But whoever rejects the Son of God will never experience the life that God desires for them, and they remain under God's judgment."

JOHN CHAPTER 4

When Jesus realized that the Pharisees were aware He was gaining and baptizing more followers than John—though Jesus Himself wasn't baptizing, but His disciples were—He left Judea and returned to Galilee. On the way, He had to pass through Samaria.

He came to a Samaritan town called Sychar, near the land that Jacob had given to his son Joseph. Jacob's well was there, and Jesus, tired from His journey, sat down by the well. It was about noon.

A Samaritan woman came to draw water, and Jesus said to her, "Will you give me a drink?" (His disciples had gone into town to buy food.)

Surprised, the woman said, "You're a Jew, and I am a Samaritan woman. How can you ask me for a drink?" (Jews did not associate with Samaritans.)

Jesus replied, "If you knew the gift of God and who it is that is asking you for a drink, you would have asked Him, and He would've given you living water."

The woman said, "Sir, you don't even have a bucket, and this well is deep. Where will you get this living water? Are you greater than our ancestor Jacob, who gave us this well and drank from it himself, along with his sons and his livestock?"

Jesus answered, "Anyone who drinks this water will be thirsty again, but whoever drinks the water I give will never thirst. The water I give will become a spring inside them, welling up to eternal life."

The woman said, "Sir, give me this water so I won't get thirsty and have to keep coming here to draw water."

Jesus told her, "Go, call your husband and come back."

She said, "I don't have a husband."

Jesus said, "You're right when you say you don't have a husband. You have had five husbands, and the man you are with now is not your husband. What you have said is true."

Amazed, the woman said, "Sir, I can see that you are a prophet. Our ancestors worshiped on this mountain, but you Jews claim that the place where we must worship is in Jerusalem."

Jesus said, "Believe me, a time is coming when you will worship the Father neither on this mountain nor in Jerusalem. You Samaritans worship what you do not know; we worship what we know, for salvation comes from the Jews. But a time is coming—and is now here—when true worshipers will worship the Father in Spirit and in truth. These are the kinds of worshipers the Father seeks. God is Spirit, and His worshipers must worship in Spirit and in truth."

The woman said, "I know the Messiah is coming. And when He comes, the Messiah will explain everything to us."

Jesus declared, "I, the one speaking to you, am He."

At that moment, His disciples returned. They were surprised to find Jesus talking with a woman, but no one asked, "What do you want?" or "Why are You talking with her?"

The woman left her water jar, hurried back to town, and said to the people, "Come and see a man who told me everything I ever did. Could this be the Messiah?" They came out of the town and made their way toward Jesus.

Meanwhile, the disciples urged Jesus, "Rabbi, eat something."

But He said, "I have food to eat that you do not know about."

Confused, the disciples asked one another, "Did someone bring Him food?"

Jesus explained, "My food is to do the will of the One who sent Me and to finish God's work. Don't you say, 'Four more months, and then it's harvest time'? Look around! The fields are ripe for harvest. The one who reaps receives wages and gathers fruit for eternal life, so the sower and the reaper can rejoice together. That saying is true: 'One sows, and another reaps.' I sent you to reap what you did not work for. Others have done the hard work, and you have benefited from their labor."

Many Samaritans from the town believed in Jesus because of the woman's testimony: "He told me everything I ever did." When they came to Him, they urged Him to stay, and He stayed for two days. Many more believed because of what He said. They told the woman, "Now we believe, not just because of what you said, but because we heard Him for ourselves. We know this man really is the Savior of the world."

After two days, Jesus left for Galilee. He had said before that a prophet is not honored in his hometown. Yet when Jesus arrived in Galilee, the people welcomed Him because they had seen everything that He did in Jerusalem at the Passover festival.

Once again, Jesus visited Cana in Galilee, where He had turned water into wine. A royal official there had a son in Capernaum who was very sick. When the man heard that Jesus had arrived, he went to Him and begged Him to come heal his son, who was about to die.

Jesus said, "Unless you see signs and wonders, you will not believe."

The official pleaded, "Sir, come before my child dies."

Jesus told him, "Go. Your son will live." The man believed what Jesus said and left.

On his way home, his servants met him with news: "Your son is alive!" He asked when his son got better, and they told him, "Yesterday, at one in the afternoon, the fever left him." The father realized this was the exact time Jesus said, "Your son will live." So, he and his whole household believed.

This was the second miraculous sign Jesus performed after coming from Judea to Galilee.

JOHN CHAPTER 5

After this, there was a Jewish feast, and Jesus went up to Jerusalem. In Jerusalem, near the Sheep Gate, there was a pool called Bethesda, which had five covered porches. A large crowd of sick people—those who were blind, lame, or paralyzed—would gather there, waiting for the water to move. From time to time, an angel would come and stir the water, and the first person to step in after the water was stirred would be healed of their disease.

One man had been there for thirty-eight years. He was unable to walk. When Jesus saw him lying there and realized how long he had been in that condition, He asked, "Do you want to get well?"

The man replied, "Sir, I have no one to help me into the pool when the water is stirred. While I am trying to get in, someone else always gets there ahead of me."

Jesus said to him, "Get up! Pick up your mat and walk." Immediately, the man was healed. He picked up his mat and started walking. This happened on the Sabbath.

Some Jewish leaders saw the man and said, "It's the Sabbath! You're not allowed to carry your mat."

He replied, "The man who healed me told me to pick up my mat and walk."

They asked him, "Who told you to do that?" But the man did not know who it was, because Jesus had slipped away into the crowd.

Later, Jesus found the man in the temple and said, "See, you are well now. Stop sinning, or something worse may happen to you." The man went and told the Jewish leaders that it was Jesus who had healed him.

Because of this, the Jewish leaders began to persecute Jesus. They wanted to kill Him because He was doing these things on the Sabbath. But Jesus said, "My Father is always at work, and so am I." This made the Jewish leaders even more determined to kill Him. Not only was He breaking the Sabbath, but He was also calling God His Father, making Himself equal with God.

Jesus responded, "I tell you the truth, the Son can do nothing by Himself. He only does what He sees the Father doing. Whatever the Father does, the Son also does. The Father loves the Son and shows Him everything He does. The Father will show Him even greater works than these, so you will be amazed. Just as the Father raises the dead and gives them life, the Son also gives life to whoever He chooses. Moreover, the Father doesn't judge anyone but has entrusted all judgment to the Son, so that everyone will honor the Son just as they honor the Father. Anyone who does not honor the Son does not honor the Father who sent Him.

"I am telling you the truth: Whoever hears my words and believes in the One who sent me has eternal life. They've crossed over from death to life and will not be condemned. A time is coming—and is already here—when the dead will hear the voice of the Son of God, and those who hear will live. For as the Father has life in Himself, He has also given the Son life in Himself. He has given Him the authority to judge because He is the Son of Man.

"Don't be amazed by this, because a time is coming when everyone in their graves will hear His voice and come out. Those who have done good will rise to life, and those who have done evil will rise to be condemned. I can do nothing by myself. I judge only as I hear, and my judgment is fair because I don't seek my own will but the will of the One who sent me.

"If I testify about myself, my testimony isn't valid. But there's another who testifies about me, and I know His testimony is true. You sent people to John, and he testified to the truth. I don't rely on human testimony, but I mention this so that you may be saved. John was a burning and shining light, and for a time, you were happy to bask in his light.

"But I have a greater testimony than John's. The works the Father has given me to accomplish—the very works I am do-ing—testify that the Father has sent me. And the Father who sent me has Himself testified about me. You have never heard His voice or seen His form, and His word does not dwell in you because you do not believe the One He sent.

"You search the Scriptures because you think they give you eternal life, but those very Scriptures point to me! Yet you refuse to come to me for life. I don't accept praise from people, but I know you. I know you don't have the love of God in your hearts. I have come in my Father's name, and you don't accept me. But if someone else comes in their own name, you'll accept them. How can you believe when you seek praise from one another and make no effort to seek the praise that comes from the only true God?

"Don't think I will accuse you before the Father. Your accuser is Moses, the one you've put your hope in. If you believed Moses, you would believe me, because he wrote about me. But since you don't believe what he wrote, how will you believe what I say?"

JOHN CHAPTER 6

A fter this, Jesus crossed over the Sea of Galilee, also known as the Sea of Tiberias. A large crowd followed Him because they had seen the miracles He performed, healing the sick. Jesus went up a mountainside and sat down with His disciples. It was almost time for the Jewish Passover feast.

As Jesus looked out, He saw a great crowd coming toward Him. He turned to Philip and asked, "Where can we buy bread to feed all these people?" (He already knew what He was going to do, but He asked to test Philip's faith.)

Philip replied, "Even eight months' wages wouldn't be enough to buy bread for everyone to have even a little."

Andrew, Simon Peter's brother, spoke up: "There's a boy here with five barley loaves and two small fish, but what good is that for so many people?"

Jesus said, "Have the people sit down." The area was covered with grass, and about five thousand men sat down. Jesus took the loaves, gave thanks, and distributed them to the crowd. He did the same with the fish, and everyone ate as much as they wanted.

When they were full, Jesus told His disciples, "Gather the leftovers so nothing is wasted." They collected twelve baskets of leftover bread from the five barley loaves.

When the people saw this miracle, they said, "Surely this is the Prophet who is to come into the world!" But Jesus knew they were about to come and make Him king by force, so He withdrew to a mountain alone.

That evening, His disciples went down to the lake, got into a boat, and set off across the sea toward Capernaum. By now it was dark, and Jesus had not yet joined them. A strong wind began to blow, and the waters grew rough. After rowing three or four miles, they saw Jesus walking on the water, coming toward the boat, and they were terrified. But Jesus said, "It's me; don't be afraid." They welcomed Him into the boat, and immediately they reached the shore.

The next day, the crowd that had stayed on the far side of the lake realized Jesus and His disciples were gone. They got into boats, crossed the lake, and found Him in Capernaum. "Rabbi, when did you get here?" they asked.

Jesus replied, "You're looking for me not because you saw the signs I performed, but because you ate the bread and were satisfied. Don't work for food that spoils; instead, work for food that lasts forever, which the Son of Man will give you. For on Him, God the Father has placed His seal of approval."

They asked, "What must we do to do the works God requires?"

Jesus answered, "The work of God is this: to believe in the One He has sent."

They said, "What sign will You give us so we can see and believe? Our ancestors ate manna in the wilderness, as it's written: 'He gave them bread from heaven to eat.'"

Jesus said, "It wasn't Moses who gave you bread from heaven; it's My Father who gives you the true bread from heaven. The bread of God is the One who comes down from heaven and gives life to the world."

"Lord," they said, "always give us this bread."

Jesus declared, "I am the bread of life. Whoever comes to Me will never go hungry, and whoever believes in Me will never be thirsty. But as I have told you, you have seen Me and still you do not believe. All those the Father gives Me will come to Me, and I will not turn anyone away. I've come down from heaven, not to do My own will, but the will of Him who sent Me. And His will is that I won't lose anyone He has given Me, but will raise them up on the last day. Everyone who looks to the Son and believes in Him will have eternal life, and I will raise them up at the last day."

The crowd began to grumble. "Isn't this Jesus, the son of Joseph? We know His parents. How can He say, 'I came down from heaven'?"

Jesus replied, "Stop complaining. No one can come to Me unless the Father draws them, and I will raise them up at the last day. It is written in the prophets: 'They will all be taught by God.' Everyone who listens to the Father and learns from Him comes to Me. No one has seen the Father except the One who is from God; only He has seen the Father. I am telling you the truth: whoever believes in Me has eternal life. I am the bread of life. Your ancestors ate manna in the wilderness, and they died. But here is the bread that comes down from heaven, so anyone may eat it and not die. I am the living bread that came down from heaven. Whoever eats this bread will live forever. This bread is My flesh, which I will give for the life of the world."

The people argued, "How can this man give us His flesh to eat?"

Jesus said, "Unless you eat the flesh of the Son of Man and drink His blood, you have no life in you. Whoever eats My flesh and drinks My blood has eternal life, and I will raise them up at the last day. My flesh is real food, and My blood is real drink. Whoever eats My flesh and drinks My blood remains in Me, and I in them. Just as I live because of the Father, so the one who feeds on this bread will live because of Me. This is the bread that came down from heaven. Unlike your ancestors, who ate manna and died, whoever eats this bread will live forever."

Hearing this, many disciples said, "This is hard to accept. Who can understand it?"

Knowing their thoughts, Jesus said, "Does this offend you? What if you see the Son of Man ascend to where He was before? The Spirit gives life; the flesh counts for nothing. The words I've spoken to you are full of Spirit and life. But some of you don't believe."

From this point, many disciples turned back and no longer followed Him. Jesus asked the Twelve, "Do you want to leave too?"

Simon Peter answered, "Lord, where else would we go? You alone have the words of eternal life. We have come to believe and know that You are the Holy One of God."

Jesus replied, "Did not I choose you, the Twelve? Yet one of you is a devil." He was referring to Judas Iscariot, who would later betray Him.

JOHN CHAPTER 7

After this, Jesus stayed in Galilee, avoiding Judea because the Jewish leaders were looking for a way to kill Him. The Jewish Feast of Tabernacles was approaching, and His brothers said to Him, "You should leave here and go to Judea so Your disciples can see the amazing things You're doing. No one works in secret when he wants to be famous. If You are doing these miracles, show Yourself to the world." (Even His brothers did not believe in Him at this point.)

Jesus replied, "The right time for Me has not yet come, but for you, any time is right. The world can't hate you, but it hates Me because I tell the truth about its evil deeds. You go on to the feast. I am not going yet because My time has not fully come." After saying this, He stayed in Galilee.

However, after His brothers left for the feast, Jesus also went—secretly, without drawing attention to Himself. At the feast, the Jewish leaders were looking for Him and asking, "Where is He?" Among the crowds, there was a lot of whispered discussion about Him. Some said, "He's a good man." Others argued, "No, He's deceiving the people." But no one spoke about Him openly because they were afraid of the Jewish leaders.

Halfway through the feast, Jesus went up to the temple courts and began to teach. The people were amazed and asked, "How did this man gain such learning without having studied?"

Jesus answered, "My teaching is not My own. It comes from the One who sent Me. Anyone who chooses to do the will of God will know whether My teaching is from God, or if I am speaking on My own. Whoever speaks on their own seeks their own glory. But the one who seeks the glory of the One who sent Him, He is truthful, and there's nothing false in Him. Did not Moses give you the law? Yet none of you keeps the law. Why are you trying to kill Me?"

"You're demon-possessed!" the crowd shouted. "Who's trying to kill You?"

Jesus said, "I did one miracle, and you were all amazed. But because Moses gave you the law of circumcision (though it actually came from the patriarchs), you circumcise a boy on the Sabbath. If a boy can be circumcised on the Sabbath so the law of Moses isn't broken, why are you angry with Me for healing an entire man on the Sabbath? Stop judging by mere appearances and judge correctly."

Some of the people of Jerusalem began to ask, "Isn't this the man they are trying to kill? Yet here He is, speaking openly, and they aren't saying a word to Him. Have the authorities really concluded that He is the Messiah? But we know where this man is from; when the Messiah comes, no one will know where He's from."

Then Jesus, still teaching in the temple courts, cried out, "Yes, you know Me, and you know where I am from. I have not come on My own, but the One who sent Me is true. You don't know Him, but I know Him because I am from Him, and He sent Me."

At this, they tried to seize Him, but no one could lay a hand on Him because His time had not yet come. Still, many in the crowd believed in Him and said, "When the Messiah comes, will He perform more signs than this man?"

The Pharisees heard the crowd whispering these things about Him, so they and the chief priests sent temple guards to arrest Him. Jesus said, "I am with you for only a short time, and then, I am going to the One who sent Me. You will look for Me, but you won't find Me; where I am, you cannot come."

The people were puzzled. "Where does He plan to go that we can't find Him? Will He go to our people scattered among the Greeks and teach the Gentiles? What does He mean by saying, 'You'll look for Me, but you won't find Me,' and 'Where I am, you cannot come'?"

On the last and greatest day of the feast, Jesus stood and said in a loud voice, "If anyone is thirsty, let them come to Me and drink. Whoever believes in Me, as Scripture has said, rivers of living water will flow from within them." (By this, He meant the Spirit, whom those who believed in Him would later receive. The Spirit had not yet been given because Jesus had not yet been glorified.)

When the people heard this, some said, "Surely this man is the Prophet." Others said, "He's the Messiah." Still, others asked, "How can the Messiah come from Galilee? Doesn't Scripture say the Messiah will come from David's descendants and Bethlehem, the town where David lived?" So, the people were divided because of Him. Some wanted to seize Him, but no one laid a hand on Him.

Finally, the temple guards went back to the chief priests and Pharisees, who asked, "Why didn't you bring Him in?"

"No one ever spoke the way that this man does," the guards replied.

"You mean He has deceived you also?" the Pharisees retorted. "Have any of the rulers or Pharisees believed in Him? No! But this mob, who knows nothing of the law—there's a curse on them."

Nicodemus, who had gone to Jesus earlier and was one of their own number, asked, "Does our law condemn a man without first hearing him to find out what he is doing?"

They replied, "Are you from Galilee, too? Look into it, and you will find that no prophet comes out of Galilee."

Then they all went home.

JOHN CHAPTER 8

J esus went to the Mount of Olives, and early in the morning, He returned to the temple. Crowds of people gathered around Him, and He sat down to teach them.

While He was teaching, the scribes and Pharisees brought a woman caught in the act of adultery and made her stand before everyone. They said to Him, "Teacher, this woman was caught in the very act of adultery. The law of Moses commands us to stone such women. What do You say?" They said this to trap Him, so they could establish grounds to accuse Him.

But Jesus bent down and began writing on the ground with His finger, as if He did not hear them. They kept pressing Him for an answer, so He stood and said, "Let the one who is without sin cast the first stone." Then He bent down again and continued writing on the ground.

One by one, the people who heard Him began to leave, starting with the oldest. When Jesus and the woman were the only ones left, Jesus straightened up and asked her, "Where are your accusers? Has no one condemned you?"

"No one, Lord," she replied.

Jesus said, "Then neither do I condemn you. Go now and leave your life of sin."

Later, Jesus spoke to the people, saying, "I am the light of the world. Whoever follows Me will never walk in darkness but will have the light of life."

The Pharisees objected, "You're testifying about Yourself, so Your testimony isn't valid."

Jesus replied, "Even if I testify about Myself, My testimony is valid because I know where I came from and where I am going. But you don't know where I come from or where I am going. You judge by human standards, but I judge no one. And if I do judge, My decisions are true because I am not alone—I stand with the Father who sent Me. Your own law says the testimony of two witnesses is valid. I am one witness, and My Father, who sent Me, is the other."

They asked Him, "Where is Your Father?"

Jesus answered, "You don't know Me or My Father. If you knew Me, you would know My Father also."

He spoke these words while teaching in the temple courts near the treasury, but no one arrested Him because His time had not yet come.

Jesus continued, "I am going away, and you will look for Me, but you will die in your sin. Where I go, you cannot come."

The people asked, "Is He planning to kill Himself? Is that why He says, 'Where I go, you cannot come'?"

Jesus said, "You are from below; I am from above. You are of this world; I am not of this world. That's why I told you that you will die in your sins. Unless you believe that I am who I say I am, then you will die in your sins."

They asked, "Who are You?"

Jesus replied, "Just what I've been saying all along. I have much to say in judgment of you, but the One who sent Me is truthful, and I speak what I've heard from Him."

They did not understand that He was talking about the Father, so Jesus said, "When you have lifted up the Son of Man, then you will know that I am the One that I claim to be, and that I do nothing on My own but speak just what the Father has taught Me. The One who sent Me is with Me; He has not left Me alone, for I always do what pleases Him." Many who heard Him say this believed in Him.

Jesus said to those who believed, "If you hold to My teaching, you are truly My disciples. Then you will know the truth, and the truth will set you free."

They answered, "We are Abraham's descendants and have never been slaves to anyone. How can You say that we will be set free?"

Jesus replied, "I tell you the truth, everyone who sins is a slave to sin. A slave has no permanent place in the family, but a son belongs to it forever. If the Son sets you free, you will be free indeed. I know you are Abraham's descendants, but you are trying to kill Me because My word has no place in you. I am telling you what I have seen in the Father's presence. And you do what you have heard from your father."

They claimed, "Abraham is our father."

Jesus said, "If you were Abraham's children, you would do what Abraham did. But you're trying to kill Me—a man who has told you the truth—the truth that I heard from God. Abraham didn't do that. You're doing the works of your real father."

They protested, "We're not illegitimate children. We have one Father—God Himself."

Jesus said, "If God were your Father, you would love Me because I came from God. I did not come on My own; He sent Me. Why don't you understand what I am saying? You don't understand, because you cannot accept My word. You belong to your father, the devil, and you want to carry out his desires. He was a murderer from the beginning and he does not stand in the truth because there is no truth in him. When he lies, he speaks his native language, for he is a liar and the father of lies. Yet because I tell you the truth, you don't believe Me. Can any of you prove Me guilty of sin? If I am telling the truth, why don't you believe Me? Whoever belongs to God hears what God says. The reason you don't hear, is because you don't belong to God."

The people accused Him, "Aren't we right in saying You are a Samaritan and demon-possessed?"

"I am not demon-possessed," Jesus replied. "I honor My Father, but you dishonor Me. I am not seeking glory for Myself, but only God seeks the Glory, and He is the judge. I tell you the truth, whoever obeys My word will never see death."

They retorted, "Now we know You're demon-possessed! Abraham died, and so did the prophets, yet You say that whoever obeys Your word will never taste death. Are You greater than our father Abraham? He died, and so did the prophets. Who do You think You are?"

Jesus said, "If I glorify Myself, My glory means nothing. My Father, whom you claim as your God, is the one who glorifies Me. Though you don't know Him, I know Him. If I said I did not, I'd be a liar like you. But I do know Him and I obey His word.

Your father Abraham rejoiced at the thought of seeing My day; he saw it and was glad."

They said, "You're not even fifty years old, and You have seen Abraham?"

Jesus declared, "I tell you the truth, before Abraham was born, I am!"

At this, they picked up stones to stone Him, but Jesus hid Himself and slipped away from the temple.

JOHN CHAPTER 9

As Jesus walked along, He saw a man who had been blind since birth. His disciples asked Him, "Teacher, who sinned—this man or his parents—that he was born blind?"

Jesus replied, "Neither this man nor his parents sinned. This happened so that the works of God might be displayed in him. While it's still daytime, we must do the work of the One who sent Me. Night is coming, when no one can work. As long as I am in the world, I am the light of the world."

After saying this, Jesus spat on the ground, made some mud with His saliva, and placed it on the man's eyes. "Go," He told him, "wash in the Pool of Siloam" (which means "Sent"). So the man went and washed, and he came back seeing clearly for the first time.

His neighbors and those who had seen him begging asked, "Isn't this the man who used to sit and beg?" Some said, "Yes, it's him," while others said, "No, it just looks like him." But the man himself insisted, "Yes, that was me."

"How then were your eyes opened?" they asked.

He answered, "The man called Jesus made mud, put it on my eyes, and told me to go to Siloam and wash. So I went, washed, and now I can see."

"Where is He?" they asked.

"I don't know," he replied.

They brought the man who had been blind to the Pharisees. Now it was the Sabbath when Jesus made the mud and healed him. The Pharisees also asked him how he had received his sight. He told them, "He put mud on my eyes, I washed, and now I see."

Some of the Pharisees said, "This man isn't from God because He doesn't keep the Sabbath." But others said, "How can a sinner perform such miracles?" So there was division among them.

They asked the man again, "What do you say about Him, since He opened your eyes?"

"He is a prophet," the man replied.

The Jewish leaders still did not believe that the man had been blind and gained his sight, so they called his parents. "Is this your son?" they asked. "Is this the one you say was born blind? How is it that he can see now?"

His parents answered, "We know this is our son and that he was born blind. But how he can see now, or who opened his eyes, we don't know. Ask him. He's of age; he can speak for himself." They said this because they were afraid of the Jewish leaders, who had already decided that anyone who acknowledged that Jesus was the Messiah would be expelled from the synagogue. That's why his parents said, "He's of age; ask him."

The leaders called the man back and said, "Give glory to God by telling the truth. We know this man is a sinner."

The man replied, "Whether He's a sinner or not, I don't know. One thing I do know: I was blind, but now I see!"

They asked him again, "What did He do to you? How did He open your eyes?"

He answered, "I've already told you, and you have not listened. Why do you want to hear it again? Do you want to become His disciples too?"

They insulted him and said, "You're His disciple! We're disciples of Moses. We know that God spoke to Moses, but as for this fellow, we don't even know where He comes from."

The man answered, "Now that is remarkable! You don't know where He comes from, yet He opened my eyes. We know that God doesn't listen to sinners, but He listens to the godly person who does His will. Nobody has ever heard of someone opening the eyes of a man born blind. If this man were not from God, He could do nothing."

To this, they replied, "You were steeped in sin at birth; how dare you lecture us!" And they threw him out.

When Jesus heard that they had cast the man out, He found him and said, "Do you believe in the Son of God?"

The man asked, "Who is He, Lord, so that I may believe in Him?"

Jesus said, "You have now seen Him. In fact, He is the one speaking with you."

The man said, "Lord, I believe," and he worshipped Him.

Jesus said, "For judgment I have come into this world, so that the blind will see, and those who see will become blind."

Some Pharisees were with Jesus, heard what He said, and they asked, "Are we blind too?"

Jesus replied, "If you were blind, you wouldn't be guilty of sin. But since you claim that you can see, your guilt remains."

JOHN CHAPTER 10

J esus said, "Truly, I tell you, anyone who doesn't enter the sheep pen through the gate, but climbs in some other way, he is a thief and a robber. The one who enters by the gate is the shepherd of the sheep. The gatekeeper opens the gate for the shepherd, and the sheep listen to his voice. He calls his own sheep by name and leads them out. When he has brought out all his own, the shepherd goes ahead of them, and the sheep follow him because they know his voice. But they will never follow a stranger; instead, they will run away from him because they do not recognize a stranger's voice."

Jesus shared this illustration, but the people didn't understand what He meant. So He explained again: "I tell you the truth, I am the gate for the sheep. All who came before Me were thieves and robbers, but the sheep didn't listen to them. I am the gate; whoever enters through Me will be saved. They will come in and go out and find pasture. The thief comes only to steal, kill, and destroy; I have come that they may have life, and have it abundantly.

"I am the good shepherd. The good shepherd lays down His life for the sheep. The hired hand, who isn't the shepherd and doesn't own the sheep, abandons the sheep and runs away when he sees the wolf coming. Then the wolf attacks and scatters the flock. The hired hand runs away because he doesn't care about the sheep. I am the good shepherd. I know My sheep, and My sheep know Me—just as the Father knows Me, and I know the Father. I lay down My life for the sheep.

"I have other sheep that are not of this sheep pen. I must bring them also. They too will listen to My voice, and there will be one flock and one shepherd. The Father loves Me because I lay down My life—only to take it up again. No one takes it from Me, but I lay My life down on My own accord. I have the authority to lay it down and I have the authority to take it up again. This command I received from My Father."

These words caused division among the people. Many said, "He's demon-possessed and out of His mind. Why listen to Him?" But others argued, "These are not the words of a demon-possessed man. Can a demon open the eyes of the blind?"

It was winter, and the Feast of Dedication was taking place in Jerusalem. Jesus was walking in the temple courts, in Solomon's Colonnade, when some people surrounded Him and said, "How long will You keep us in suspense? If You are the Messiah, tell us plainly."

Jesus replied, "I have told you, but you don't believe. The works I do in My Father's name testify about Me, but you don't believe, because you are not My sheep. My sheep listen to My voice; I know them, and they follow Me. I give them eternal life, and they will never perish. No one can snatch them out of My hand. My Father, who has given them to Me, is greater than all; no one can snatch them out of My Father's hand. I and the Father are one."

At this, they picked up stones to stone Him. But Jesus said, "I have shown you many good works from the Father. For which of these do you stone Me?"

They answered, "We are not stoning You for any good work but for blasphemy, because You, a mere man, claim to be God."

Jesus responded, "Isn't it written in your law, 'I have said you are gods'? If He called them 'gods,' to whom the word of God came—and Scripture cannot be broken—what about the One whom the Father set apart as His very own and sent into the world? Why then do you accuse Me of blasphemy because I said, 'I am God's Son'? Don't believe Me unless I do the works of My Father. But if I do the works of my Father, even if you don't believe Me, believe the works that I do, so that you may know and understand that the Father is in Me, and I am in the Father."

Again, they tried to seize Him, but He escaped their grasp and went back across the Jordan River to the place where John had been baptizing earlier. He stayed there, and many people came to Him. They said, "John didn't perform any miracles, but everything he said about this man was true." And many that were in that place, put their faith in Jesus.

JOHN CHAPTER 11

A man named Lazarus, from the village of Bethany, was very sick. He was the brother of Mary and Martha. (This was the same Mary who later anointed the Lord with perfume and wiped His feet with her hair.) The sisters sent a message to Jesus: "Lord, the one You love is sick."

When Jesus heard this, He said, "This sickness will not end in death. No, this is for God's glory, so that the Son of God may be glorified through it." Jesus loved Martha, Mary, and Lazarus deeply. Yet, when He heard that Lazarus was sick, He stayed where He was for two more days.

Then He said to His disciples, "Let's go back to Judea."

"But Rabbi," they objected, "a short while ago the Jews there tried to stone You, and now You want to go back?"

Jesus answered, "Are there not twelve hours of daylight? Anyone who walks in the daytime will not stumble, for they see by this world's light. But if they walk at night, they stumble, because they have no light." After He said this, He added, "Our friend Lazarus has fallen asleep, but I am going to wake him up."

His disciples said, "Lord, if he's sleeping, he will get better." They didn't realize Jesus was speaking about Lazarus's death, so He told them plainly, "Lazarus is dead. And for your sake, I am glad I wasn't there, so you may believe. But now, let's go to him."

Then Thomas, also called Didymus, said to the others, "Let's go too, that we may die with Him."

When Jesus arrived in Bethany, Lazarus had already been in the tomb for four days. Bethany was close to Jerusalem, just under two miles away, and many people had come to comfort Martha and Mary in their loss. When Martha heard that Jesus was coming, she went out to meet Him, but Mary stayed at home.

"Lord," Martha said to Jesus, "if You had been here, my brother would not have died. But I know that even now God will give You whatever You ask."

Jesus said to her, "Your brother will rise again."

Martha replied, "I know he will rise again in the resurrection—at the last day."

Jesus said to her, "I am the resurrection and the life. Anyone who believes in Me will live, even though they die; and whoever lives and believes in Me will never die. Do you believe this?"

"Yes, Lord," she replied. "I believe that You are the Messiah, the Son of God, who has come into the world."

After she said this, she went back and called her sister Mary aside. "The Teacher is here," she said, "and He's asking for you." Mary got up quickly and went to Him. Jesus had not yet entered the village but was still at the place where Martha had met Him. When the people who were comforting Mary saw her leave suddenly, they followed her, thinking she was going to mourn at the tomb.

When Mary reached Jesus, she fell at His feet and said, "Lord, if You had been here, my brother would not have died." When Jesus saw her weeping, and the people with her also weeping, He was deeply moved in spirit and troubled.

"Where have you laid him?" He asked.

"Come and see, Lord," they replied.

Jesus wept.

The people said, "See how much He loved him!" But others said, "Couldn't He, who opened the eyes of the blind, have kept this man from dying?"

Jesus, once more deeply moved, came to the tomb. It was a cave with a stone laid across the entrance. "Take away the stone," He said.

"But Lord," said Martha, "by now there's a bad odor, for he's been in there four days."

Jesus replied, "Didn't I tell you that if you believe, you will see the glory of God?"

So they took the stone away. Then Jesus looked up and said, "Father, I thank You that You have heard Me. I know that You always hear Me, but I said this for the benefit of the people standing here, so they may believe that You sent Me."

After He said this, Jesus called out in a loud voice, "Lazarus, come out!"

The dead man came out, his hands and feet wrapped with strips of linen, and a cloth around his face. Jesus said, "Take off the grave clothes and let him go."

Many of the people who had come to comfort Mary saw what Jesus did and believed in Him. But some went to the Pharisees and told them what Jesus had done. Then the chief priests and Pharisees called a meeting. "What are we accomplishing?" they asked. "This man is performing many signs. If we let Him go on, everyone will believe in Him, and then the Romans will come and take away both our temple and our nation."

Caiaphas, the high priest that year, said, "You know nothing at all! Don't you realize it's better for one man to die for the people than for the whole nation to perish?" He didn't say this on his own but prophesied that Jesus would die for the Jewish nation—and not only for them, but also for all the children of God scattered around the world, and Jesus would bring them together.

From that day, they plotted to take Jesus's life. So Jesus no longer moved about publicly among the Jews. Instead, He withdrew to a region near the wilderness, to a village called Ephraim, where He stayed with His disciples.

As the Jewish Passover approached, many people went to Jerusalem to purify themselves. They kept looking for Jesus and wondered, "What do you think? Isn't He coming to the Passover festival?" But the chief priests and Pharisees had given orders that anyone who knew where He was should report it, so they could arrest Him.

JOHN CHAPTER 12

S ix days before the Passover, Jesus arrived in Bethany, the village of Lazarus, the man He had raised from the dead. A dinner was held in Jesus's honor. Martha served the meal, while Lazarus reclined at the table with Him. Mary took a pound of expensive perfume made of pure nard, anointed Jesus's feet, and wiped His feet with her hair. The house was filled with the fragrance of the perfume.

Judas Iscariot, one of Jesus's disciples (the one who would later betray Him), objected, "Why wasn't this perfume sold and the money given to the poor? It was worth a year's wages." He didn't say this because he cared about the poor, but because he was a thief; he kept the money bag and often helped himself to what was in it.

Jesus said, "Leave her alone. She has kept this for the day of My burial. You will always have the poor among you, but you won't always have Me."

A large crowd of Jews found out that Jesus was there, and they came, not just to see Him, but also to see Lazarus, whom

Jesus had raised from the dead. The chief priests, however, plotted to kill Lazarus as well, because his resurrection was leading many people to believe in Jesus.

The next day, the crowd that had come for the feast, heard that Jesus was on His way to Jerusalem. They took palm branches and went out to meet Him, shouting, "Hosanna! Blessed is He who comes in the name of the Lord! Blessed is the King of Israel!" Jesus found a young donkey and sat on it, fulfilling the prophecy: *"Do not be afraid, Daughter Zion; see, your King is coming, seated on a donkey's colt."*

At first, the disciples didn't understand these events. Only after Jesus was glorified, did they realize these things had been written about Him—and that they had participated in fulfilling prophecy. The crowd that had witnessed Jesus raise Lazarus from the dead continued to spread the word. Many people went out to meet Him because they had heard about this miracle. The Pharisees said to one another, "Look, this is getting us nowhere. See how the whole world is following Him!"

Among those who had come to worship at the feast were some Greeks. They approached Philip, who was from Bethsaida in Galilee, and said, "Sir, we want to see Jesus." Philip told Andrew, and together they went to tell Jesus.

Jesus replied, "The hour has come for the Son of Man to be glorified. Truly, I tell you, unless a kernel of wheat falls to the ground and dies, it remains only a single seed. But if it dies, it produces many seeds. Anyone who loves their life will lose it, while anyone who hates their life in this world, will have eternal life. Whoever serves Me must follow Me, and where I am, My servant will also be. My Father will honor the one who serves Me.

"Now My soul is troubled. What shall I say—'Father, save Me from this hour'? No, it was for this very reason I came to this hour. Father, glorify Your name!"

Then a voice came from heaven: "I have glorified it, and I will glorify it again." The crowd heard the voice from heaven and said it had thundered; others said an angel had spoken to Him.

Jesus said, "This voice was for your benefit, not Mine. Now is the time for judgment on this world; now the prince of this world will be driven out. And I, when I am lifted up from the earth, will draw all people to Myself." He said this to indicate the kind of death He was going to die.

The crowd spoke up, "We have heard from the Law, that the Messiah will remain forever. How can You say the Son of Man must be lifted up? Who is this Son of Man?"

Jesus answered, "You are going to have the light just a little while longer. Walk while you have the light, before darkness overtakes you. Whoever walks in the dark doesn't know where they are going. Walk in the light while you have the light, so you may become children of light." After Jesus had spoken, He withdrew and hid Himself from them.

Despite all the miracles Jesus performed, many still didn't believe in Him. This fulfilled the words of Isaiah the prophet: *"Lord, who has believed our message, and to whom has the arm of the Lord been revealed?"* Isaiah also said, *"He has blinded their eyes and hardened their hearts, so they can neither see with their eyes, nor understand with their hearts, nor turn—and I would heal them.*" Isaiah said this because he saw Jesus's glory and spoke about Him.

Yet, many among the leaders believed in Him, but because of the Pharisees, they would not confess their faith for fear of being expelled from the synagogue. They loved the praise from men, more than they love praise from God.

Then Jesus cried out, "Whoever believes in Me does not believe in Me only, but in the One who sent Me. The one who sees Me sees the One who sent Me. I have come into the world as a light, so that no one who believes in Me should stay in darkness.

"If anyone hears My words but does not keep them, I do not judge that person. I didn't come to judge the world, but to save it. There is a judge for the one who rejects Me and does not accept My words; the very words I have spoken will condemn them at the last day. For I didn't speak on My own, but the Father who sent Me, commanded Me to say all that I have spoken. I know His command leads to eternal life. So whatever I say is just what the Father has told Me to say."

JOHN CHAPTER 13

Before the Passover feast, Jesus knew that His time had come to leave this world, and to return to the Father. He had always loved His own who were in the world, and He loved them to the very end.

When the evening meal was being served, the devil had already put it into the heart of Judas Iscariot, Simon's son, to betray Jesus. Jesus, knowing that the Father had placed all things under His authority, and that He had come from God and was returning to God, got up from the meal. He took off His outer robe, wrapped a towel around His waist, poured water into a basin, and began to wash His disciples' feet, drying them with the towel.

When He came to Simon Peter, Peter said, "Lord, are You going to wash my feet?"

Jesus replied, "You don't understand what I am doing now, but later you will."

Peter protested, "Lord, You will never wash my feet!"

Jesus answered, "If I don't wash you, you have no part with Me."

"Then, Lord," Peter said, "not just my feet, but also my hands and my head!"

Jesus said, "Anyone who has bathed is completely clean and only needs to wash their feet. And you are clean—though not every one of you." (He knew who would betray Him, which is why He said not all of them were clean.)

After washing their feet, He put on His robe and returned to His place. "Do you understand what I've done for you?" He asked. "You call Me 'Teacher' and 'Lord,' and rightly so, for that is what I am. If I, your Lord and Teacher, have washed your feet, you also ought to wash one another's feet. I've set you an example, so you should do to others as I have done for you. Truly, I tell you, no servant is greater than their master, nor is a messenger greater than the one who sent them. Now that you know these things, you will be blessed if you do them.

"I am not speaking about all of you. I know those I have chosen, but this is to fulfill the Scripture: 'The one who shares My bread has turned against Me.' I am telling you now, before it happens, so that when it does happen, you will believe that I am who I am. Truly, whoever accepts anyone I send, accepts Me. And whoever accepts Me, accepts the One who sent Me."

After saying this, Jesus was deeply troubled in spirit and said, "Truly, I tell you, one of you is going to betray Me."

The disciples looked at each other, unsure of whom He meant. One of His disciples, the one Jesus loved, was reclining close to Him. Simon Peter motioned to this disciple and said, "Ask Him who He means."

Leaning back against Jesus, the disciple asked, "Lord, who is it?"

Jesus replied, "It is the one to whom I give this piece of bread after I've dipped it." He dipped the bread and gave it to Judas Iscariot, the son of Simon. As soon as Judas took the bread, Satan entered into him.

Jesus told him, "What you are about to do, do it quickly." No one at the table understood why Jesus said this to him. Some thought that, because Judas was in charge of the money, Jesus was telling him to buy what was needed for the feast or to give something to the poor. Judas took the bread and went out immediately. And it was night.

After Judas left, Jesus said, "Now the Son of Man is glorified, and God is glorified in Him. If God is glorified in Him, God will glorify the Son in Himself and will glorify Him at once.

"My children, I will be with you only a little longer. You will look for Me, and just as I told the Jewish leaders, so I tell you now: where I am going, you cannot come. A new commandment I give you: Love one another. Just as I have loved you, so you must love one another. By this, everyone will know that you are My disciples, if you love one another."

Simon Peter asked, "Lord, where are You going?"

Jesus replied, "Where I am going, you cannot follow now, but you will follow later."

Peter said, "Lord, why can't I follow You now? I will lay down my life for You."

Jesus answered, "Will you really lay down your life for Me? Truly, before the rooster crows, you will deny Me three times."

JOHN CHAPTER 14

"Don't let your hearts be troubled," Jesus said. "You believe in God; believe in Me also. In My Father's house, there are many rooms. If that were not true, I would have told you. I am going there to prepare a place for you. And if I go to prepare a place for you, I'll come back and take you to be with Me, so that where I am, you can be also. You already know the way to where I am going."

Thomas said, "Lord, we don't know where You're going, so how can we know the way?"

Jesus answered, "I am the way, the truth, and the life. No one comes to the Father except through Me. If you really know Me, you know My Father as well. From now on, you do know Him and you have seen Him."

Philip said, "Lord, show us the Father, and that will be enough for us."

Jesus replied, "Philip, have I been with you so long, and yet you still don't know Me? Anyone who has seen Me has seen the Father. So how can you say, 'Show us the Father'? Don't you believe that I am in the Father and the Father is in Me? The words I speak aren't My own—they come from the Father who lives in Me and works through Me. Believe Me when I say that I am in the Father and the Father is in Me. Or at least believe because of the works you have seen.

"Truly, I tell you, whoever believes in Me will do the works I have been doing—and they will do even greater things because I am going to the Father. Whatever you ask in My name, I will do it, so that the Father may be glorified in the Son. If you ask anything in My name, I will do it.

"If you love Me, keep My commands. And I will ask the Father, and He will give you another Helper—the Spirit of truth—to be with you forever. The world cannot accept Him, because it neither sees Him nor knows Him. But you know Him, for He lives with you and will be in you. I won't leave you as orphans; I will come to you.

"In a little while, the world won't see Me anymore, but you will. Because I live, you will live also. On that day, you will realize that I am in My Father, and you are in Me, and I am in you. Whoever keeps My commands and obeys them is the one who loves Me. The one who loves Me will be loved by My Father, and I will love them and show Myself to them."

Judas (not Iscariot) said, "Lord, why do You intend to show Yourself to us and not to the world?"

Jesus replied, "Anyone who loves Me will obey My teaching. My Father will love them, and We will come to them and make Our home with them. But anyone who does not love Me won't obey My teaching. These words you hear are not My own; they belong to the Father who sent Me.

"I am telling you these things while I am still with you. But the Helper, the Holy Spirit, whom the Father will send in My Name, will teach you all things and remind you of everything I have said. Peace I leave with you; My peace I give to you. I do not give as the world gives. Do not let your hearts be troubled, and don't be afraid.

"You have heard Me say I am going away and coming back to you. If you loved Me, you would be glad that I am going to the Father, because the Father is greater than I. I have told you now before it happens so that when it does, you will believe. I will not say much more to you because the prince of this world is coming. He has no power over Me. But I do what the Father has commanded Me, so the world will know that I love the Father. Come now, let us go."

JOHN CHAPTER 15

J esus said, "I am the true vine, and My Father is the gardener. He cuts off every branch in Me that does not bear fruit, while every branch that does bear fruit He prunes so that it will be even more fruitful. You are already clean because of the word I have spoken to you. Remain in Me, as I also remain in you. Just as a branch cannot bear fruit by itself unless it remains in the vine, neither can you bear fruit unless you remain in Me.

"I am the vine, and you are the branches. If you remain in Me and I in you, you will bear much fruit; apart from Me, you can do nothing. If you do not remain in Me, you are like a branch that is thrown away and withers; such branches are picked up, thrown into the fire, and burned. But if you remain in Me and My words remain in you, ask whatever you wish, and it will be done for you. This is how My Father is glorified—that you bear much fruit, showing yourselves to be My disciples.

"As the Father has loved Me, so have I loved you. Now remain in My love. If you keep My commandments, you will remain in

My love, just as I have kept My Father's commandments and remain in His love. I have told you this so that My joy may be in you, and your joy may be complete.

"My command is this: Love one another as I have loved you. There's no greater love than to lay down one's life for one's friends. You are My friends if you do what I command. I no longer call you servants, because a servant does not know their master's business. Instead, I've called you friends, because everything I learned from My Father I have made known to you.

"You didn't choose Me; I chose you and appointed you so that you might go and bear fruit—fruit that will last—and so that whatever you ask in My name, the Father will give it to you. This is My command: Love one another.

"If the world hates you, keep in mind that it hated Me first. If you belonged to the world, the world would love you as its own. But as it is, you do not belong to the world, because I have chosen you out of the world. That's why the world hates you. Remember what I told you: A servant isn't greater than his master. If they persecuted Me, they will persecute you also. If they obeyed My teaching, they will obey yours also. They will treat you this way because of My name, for they do not know the One who sent Me.

"If I had not come and spoken to them, they wouldn't be guilty of sin. But now they have no excuse for their sin. Whoever hates Me, hates My Father as well. If I hadn't done works among them that no one else did, then they would not be guilty of sin. But now they have seen Me and they have hated both Me and My Father. This is to fulfill what is written in their law: 'They hated Me without reason.'

"When the Advocate comes, whom I'll send to you from the Father—the Spirit of truth who goes out from the Father—He will testify about Me. And you also must testify, for you have been with Me from the beginning."

JOHN CHAPTER 16

J esus said, "I've told you these things so that you will not stumble or lose faith. They will put you out of the synagogues, and the time will come when those who kill you will think they are offering a service to God. They will do this because they don't know the Father or Me. But I have warned you, so when the time comes, you will remember that I told you about it. I didn't tell you this from the beginning because I was with you.

"But now I am going back to the One who sent Me. None of you are asking, 'Where are You going?' Instead, your hearts are filled with sorrow because of what I've said. Yet I tell you the truth: It's better for you that I go away. If I don't go, the Helper won't come to you. But if I go, I will send Him to you.

"When He comes, He will convict the world of sin, righteousness, and judgment: of sin, because they don't believe in Me; of righteousness, because I am going to the Father and you will no longer see Me; and of judgment, because the ruler of this world has been condemned.

"I still have much to say to you, but you are not ready to bear it now. However, when the Spirit of truth comes, He will guide you into all truth. He won't speak on His own, but He will tell you what He hears and show you what is to come. He will glorify Me by taking what is Mine and making it known to you. Everything the Father has is Mine; that's why I said the Spirit will take from what is Mine and show it to you.

"In a little while, you won't see Me anymore, but then, after a little while, you will see Me again."

Some of the disciples said to one another, "What does He mean by saying, 'In a little while you won't see Me, and then after a little while you will see Me,' and 'I am going to the Father'? What is this 'little while'? We don't understand."

Jesus knew they wanted to ask Him, so He said, "Are you wondering what I meant when I said, 'In a little while you won't see Me, and then after a little while you will see Me'? Truly, I tell you, you will weep and mourn while the world rejoices. You will grieve, but your grief will turn to joy. A woman in labor feels pain because her time has come, but once her baby is born, she forgets the anguish because of the joy that a child has entered the world. In the same way, you are full of sorrow now, but I will see you again, and your hearts will rejoice. No one will take your joy away.

"When that day comes, you won't need to ask Me for anything. Truly, I tell you, whatever you ask the Father in My name, He will give you. Until now, you haven't asked for anything in My name. Ask, and you will receive, so your joy will be complete.

"I've been speaking to you in figures of speech, but the time is coming when I will speak plainly to you about the Father. On that day, you will ask in My name, and I am not saying that I will ask the Father on your behalf. No, the Father Himself loves you because you have loved Me and you have believed that I came from God. I came from the Father and entered the world; now I am leaving the world and going back to the Father."

Then His disciples said, "Now You are speaking plainly and not using figures of speech. Now we understand that You know all things and You don't need anyone to ask You questions. This makes us believe that You came from God."

Jesus replied, "Do you finally believe? The time is coming—and has now come—when you will be scattered, each to your own home. You will leave Me all alone. Yet I am not alone, because the Father is with Me.

"I have told you these things so that in Me you may have peace. In this world, you will have trouble. But take heart! I have overcome the world."

JOHN CHAPTER 17

After Jesus finished speaking to His disciples, He looked up toward heaven and prayed, "Father, the time has come. Glorify Your Son so that Your Son may glorify You. For You have given Him authority over all people, so He might give eternal life to all those You have entrusted to Him. And this is eternal life: that they know You, the only true God, and Jesus Christ, whom You have sent.

"I have brought You glory on earth by completing the work You gave Me to do. Now, Father, glorify Me in Your presence with the glory that I had with You before the world began.

"I have revealed Your name to those You gave Me out of the world. They were Yours; You gave them to Me, and they have obeyed Your word. Now they know that everything You have given Me comes from You. I gave them the words You gave Me, and they accepted them. They know with certainty that I came from You, and they believe that You sent Me.

"I am praying for them. I am not praying for the world, but for those You have given Me, because they are Yours. All I have is Yours, and all You have is Mine. And glory has come to Me through them.

"I will remain in the world no longer, but they are still in the world, and I am coming to You. Holy Father, protect them by the power of Your name—the name You gave Me—so that they may be one as We are one. While I was with them, I protected them and kept them safe by the name that You gave Me. None of them has been lost, except the one doomed to destruction so that Scripture would be fulfilled.

"Now I am coming to You, but I say these things while I am still in the world so that they may have the full measure of My joy within them. I have given them Your word, and the world has hated them because they are not of the world, just as I am not of the world. My prayer is not that You take them out of the world, but that You protect them from the evil one. They are not of the world, even as I am not of it. Sanctify them by the truth; Your word is truth. As You sent Me into the world, I have sent them into the world. For their sake, I sanctify Myself so that they too may be truly sanctified.

"I am not just praying for these disciples, but also for all of those who will believe in Me through their message. I pray that all of them may be one, Father, just as You are in Me, and I am in You. May they also be in Us so that the world may believe that You sent Me. I have given them the glory that You gave Me, that they may be one as We are one—I in them and You in Me—so that they may be brought to complete unity. Then the world will know that You sent Me and You have loved them even as You have loved Me.

"Father, I want those You have given Me to be with Me where I am, and to see My glory, the glory You have given Me because You loved Me before the foundation of the world.

"Righteous Father, though the world does not know You, I know You, and they know that You have sent Me. I have made You known to them and will continue to make You known, so that the love You have for Me may be in them, and that I Myself may be in them."

JOHN CHAPTER 18

After saying these things, Jesus and His disciples crossed the brook Kidron and entered a garden. This was a place Jesus often went with His disciples, so Judas, the one who betrayed Him, knew exactly where to find them. Judas came with a group of soldiers and officials sent by the chief priests and the Pharisees. They were armed with lanterns, torches, and weapons.

Knowing everything that was about to happen, Jesus stepped forward and asked, "Who are you looking for?"

They replied, "Jesus of Nazareth."

"I am He," Jesus said. And as He spoke, Judas stood there with them, and the entire group fell back to the ground.

Jesus asked them again, "Who are you looking for?"

"Jesus of Nazareth," they answered.

"I told you that I am He," Jesus replied. "If you're looking for Me, let these others go." This fulfilled His earlier words: "I have not lost any of those You gave Me."

At that moment, Simon Peter, who had a sword, drew it and struck the high priest's servant, cutting off his right ear. The servant's name was Malchus.

But Jesus said to Peter, "Put your sword away! Shall I not drink the cup the Father has given Me?"

The soldiers and officials arrested Jesus, bound Him, and took Him first to Annas, the father-in-law of Caiaphas, who was the high priest that year. Caiaphas had advised the Jewish leaders earlier that it was better for one man to die for the people.

Simon Peter and another disciple followed Jesus. The other disciple, who was known to the high priest, went into the high priest's courtyard with Jesus, but Peter waited outside at the door. The other disciple came back, spoke to the servant girl on duty, and brought Peter inside.

The servant girl at the door asked Peter, "You are not one of this man's disciples, are you?"

"I am not," Peter replied.

Meanwhile, the servants and officials stood around a fire they had made to keep warm, and Peter joined them, warming himself by the fire.

Inside, the high priest questioned Jesus about His disciples and His teaching.

"I've spoken openly to the world," Jesus replied. "I've always taught in synagogues and at the temple, where all the Jews come together. I said nothing in secret. Why question Me? Ask those who heard Me. They know what I said."

When Jesus said this, one of the officials nearby slapped Him. "Is that how you answer the high priest?" he demanded.

Jesus replied, "If I said something wrong, testify to what is wrong. But if I spoke the truth, why do you hit Me?"

Then Annas sent Him, still bound, to Caiaphas the high priest.

Meanwhile, Peter was still standing by the fire, and they asked him, "Aren't you one of His disciples too?"

Peter denied it, saying, "I am not."

One of the high priest's servants, a relative of the man whose ear Peter had cut off, challenged him, "Didn't I see you with Him in the garden?"

Again, Peter denied it, and immediately a rooster crowed.

At dawn, Jesus was taken from Caiaphas to the Roman governor's palace. The Jewish leaders didn't enter the palace, as they wanted to remain ceremonially clean to eat the Passover. So Pilate came out to them and asked, "What charges are you bringing against this man?"

"If He weren't a criminal," they replied, "we wouldn't have handed Him over to you."

Pilate said, "Take Him yourselves and judge Him by your own law."

"But we have no right to execute anyone," they objected. This fulfilled what Jesus had said about the kind of death He would die.

Pilate went back inside, summoned Jesus, and asked, "Are You the King of the Jews?"

"Is that your own idea," Jesus asked, "or did others talk to you about Me?"

"Am I a Jew?" Pilate replied. "Your own people and chief priests handed You over to me. What have You done?"

Jesus said, "My kingdom is not of this world. If it were, My servants would fight to prevent My arrest by the Jewish leaders. But now My kingdom is not from here."

"You are a king, then!" Pilate said.

Jesus answered, "You say that I am a king. In fact, the reason I was born and came into the world is to testify to the truth. Everyone on the side of truth listens to Me."

"What is truth?" Pilate retorted. Then he went out to the Jewish leaders and said, "I find no basis for a charge against Him. But it's your custom for me to release one prisoner at the Passover. Do you want me to release the King of the Jews?"

They shouted back, "No, not Him! Give us Barabbas!" (Now Barabbas had taken part in a rebellion.)

JOHN CHAPTER 19

Pilate took Jesus and had Him flogged. The soldiers twisted a crown of thorns and pressed it onto His head. They draped a purple robe around Him and mocked Him, saying, "Hail, King of the Jews!" Then they struck Him repeatedly.

Pilate went out again and told the crowd, "I am bringing Him out to you, so that you know that I find no fault in Him." Jesus stepped forward, wearing the crown of thorns and the purple robe. Pilate said, "Here is the man!"

When the chief priests and officials saw Him, they shouted, "Crucify Him! Crucify Him!"

Pilate responded, "You take Him and crucify Him. I find no basis for a charge against Him."

The Jews replied, "We have a law, and by that law, He must die because He claimed to be the Son of God." When Pilate heard this, he became even more fearful. He went back inside and asked Jesus, "Where do You come from?" But Jesus didn't answer.

"Do You refuse to speak to me?" Pilate asked. "Don't You realize I have the power to free You or crucify You?"

Jesus replied, "You would have no power over Me if it were not given to you from above. Therefore, the one who handed Me over to you is guilty of a greater sin."

From then on, Pilate tried to release Him, but the crowd kept shouting, "If you let this man go, you are no friend of Caesar! Anyone who claims to be a king opposes Caesar!"

Hearing this, Pilate brought Jesus out and sat on the judgment seat at a place called the Pavement (in Hebrew, Gabbatha). It was about noon on the day of Preparation for the Passover. Pilate said to the crowd, "Here is your King!"

But they shouted, "Take Him away! Crucify Him!"

"Shall I crucify your King?" Pilate asked.

"We have no king but Caesar," the chief priests answered.

Finally, Pilate handed Jesus over to be crucified. The soldiers took charge of Him. Carrying His own cross, Jesus went to the place called the Skull (in Hebrew, Golgotha). There they crucified Him, along with two others—one on each side, with Jesus in the middle.

Pilate had a sign fastened to the cross. It read: **JESUS OF NAZARETH, THE KING OF THE JEWS.** Many Jews read this sign because the place of crucifixion was near the city, and the sign was written in Hebrew, Latin, and Greek. The chief priests protested, "Don't write, 'The King of the Jews,' but that He claimed to be the King of the Jews."

Pilate replied, "What I have written, I have written."

When the soldiers crucified Jesus, they divided His clothes into four shares, one for each of them. They also took His seamless tunic, woven in one piece. "Let's not tear it," they said. "Let's cast lots to see who gets it." This fulfilled the Scripture: *They divided My clothes among them and cast lots for My garment.*

Near the cross stood Jesus's mother, His mother's sister, Mary the wife of Clopas, and Mary Magdalene. When Jesus saw His mother and the disciple He loved standing nearby, He said to His mother, "Woman, here is your son." Then He said to the disciple, "Here is your mother." From that moment, the disciple took Jesus's mother into his home.

Later, knowing that everything was now finished and to fulfill Scripture, Jesus said, "I am thirsty." A jar of vinegar was there, so they soaked a sponge in it, put the sponge on a hyssop branch, and lifted it to His lips. When Jesus had received the drink, He said, "It is finished." Then He bowed His head and gave up His Spirit.

Since it was the day of Preparation, the Jews didn't want the bodies left on the crosses during the Sabbath. They asked Pilate to have the legs broken and the bodies taken down. The soldiers broke the legs of the men crucified with Jesus, but when they came to Jesus, they saw that He was already dead. Instead, one of the soldiers pierced His side with a spear, and blood and water flowed out. This fulfilled Scripture: *Not one of His bones will be broken* and *They will look on the one they have pierced.*

Later, Joseph of Arimathea, a secret disciple of Jesus because he feared the Jewish leaders, asked Pilate for permission to take Jesus's body. Pilate granted it. Joseph came and took the body away. Nicodemus, who had earlier visited Jesus at night, brought a mixture of myrrh and aloes, about seventy-five pounds. Together, they wrapped Jesus's body in linen with the spices, according to Jewish burial customs.

At the place where Jesus was crucified, there was a garden with a new tomb where no one had ever been laid. Because it was the Jewish day of Preparation and the tomb was nearby, they laid Jesus there.

JOHN CHAPTER 20

Early on the first day of the week, while it was still dark, Mary Magdalene went to the tomb and saw that the stone had been rolled away from the entrance. Alarmed, she ran to find Simon Peter and the other disciple, the one Jesus loved. She exclaimed, "They have taken the Lord out of the tomb, and we don't know where they have put Him!"

Peter and the other disciple immediately set out for the tomb. They ran together, but the other disciple outran Peter and got there first. He bent down and looked inside, seeing the linen burial cloths lying there, but he didn't go in. When Peter arrived, he went straight into the tomb. He saw the linen cloths lying there, and the cloth that had been wrapped around Jesus's head, folded neatly in a separate place.

Then the other disciple, who had reached the tomb first, also went inside. He saw and believed, even though they still didn't fully understand the Scripture that said Jesus must rise from the dead. The disciples returned to their homes, puzzled.

Mary, however, stayed outside the tomb, weeping. As she bent down to look inside, she saw two angels in white, seated where Jesus's body had been—one at the head and the other at the feet. They asked her, "Woman, why are you crying?"

She replied, "They've taken my Lord away, and I don't know where they have put Him."

Turning around, she saw someone standing there but didn't realize it was Jesus. He asked her, "Woman, why are you crying? Who are you looking for?"

Thinking He was the gardener, she said, "Sir, if you have moved Him, please tell me where you have put Him, and I will take Him away."

Jesus said to her, "Mary."

Hearing her name, she turned and cried out, "Rabboni!" (which means Teacher).

Jesus told her, "Do not hold on to Me, for I have not yet ascended to the Father. Go to My brothers and tell them, 'I am ascending to My Father and your Father, to My God and your God.'"

Mary Magdalene went to the disciples with the news: "I have seen the Lord!" She told them everything He had said to her.

Later that evening, on the first day of the week, the disciples were gathered behind locked doors, fearful of the Jewish leaders. Suddenly, Jesus appeared among them and said, "Peace be with you." Then He showed them His hands and His side. The disciples were overjoyed to see the Lord.

Jesus said again, "Peace be with you! As the Father has sent Me, I am sending you." Then He breathed on them and said, "Receive the Holy Spirit. If you forgive anyone's sins, they are forgiven; if you do not forgive them, they are not forgiven."

Thomas, one of the Twelve (called Didymus), wasn't with them when Jesus appeared. When the other disciples told him, "We've seen the Lord!" he replied, "Unless I see the nail marks in His hands and put my finger where the nails were, and put my hand into His side, I will not believe."

Eight days later, the disciples were together again, and this time Thomas was with them. Even though the doors were locked, Jesus came and stood among them, saying, "Peace be with you." Then He said to Thomas, "Put your finger here; see My hands. Reach out your hand and put it into My side. Stop doubting and believe."

Thomas exclaimed, "My Lord and my God!"

Jesus responded, "Because you have seen Me, you have believed; blessed are those who have not seen me, and yet believe."

Jesus performed many other miraculous signs in the presence of His disciples, which are not recorded in this book. But these have been written so that you may believe that Jesus is the Messiah, the Son of God, and that by believing, you may have life in His name.

JOHN CHAPTER 21

A fter everything that had happened, Jesus revealed Himself again to His disciples by the Sea of Tiberias. This is
how it happened:

Simon Peter, Thomas (also called Didymus), Nathanael from
Cana in Galilee, the sons of Zebedee, and two other disciples
were together. Peter said, "I am going fishing."

The others replied, "We'll go with you." So they got into the
boat, but they caught nothing that night.

At dawn, Jesus stood on the shore, though the disciples
didn't realize it was Him. He called out, "Friends, have you
caught anything?"

"No," they answered.

Jesus said, "Throw your net on the right side of the boat, and
you'll find some." They did, and suddenly they couldn't haul the
net in because of the large number of fish.

Then the disciple whom Jesus loved said to Peter, "It's the
Lord!" As soon as Peter heard this, he wrapped his outer garment around him (because he had taken it off) and jumped

into the water. The other disciples followed in the boat, towing the net full of fish, because they weren't far from shore—about a hundred yards.

When they landed, they saw a fire of burning coals with fish on it, and some bread. Jesus said to them, "Bring some of the fish you have just caught."

Simon Peter climbed back into the boat and dragged the net ashore. It was full of 153 large fish, yet the net wasn't torn.

Jesus said, "Come and have breakfast." None of the disciples dared to ask, "Who are You?" They knew it was the Lord. Jesus came, took the bread, and gave it to them, along with the fish. This was the third time Jesus appeared to His disciples after He was raised from the dead.

When they finished eating, Jesus said to Simon Peter, "Simon, son of John, do you love Me more than these?"

"Yes, Lord," Peter replied, "You know that I love You."

Jesus said, "Feed My lambs."

Again Jesus asked, "Simon, son of John, do you love Me?"

Peter answered, "Yes, Lord, You know that I love You."

Jesus said, "Take care of My sheep."

A third time, Jesus said, "Simon, son of John, do you love Me?"

Peter was hurt because Jesus asked him the third time, "Do you love Me?" He said, "Lord, You know all things; You know that I love You."

Jesus said, "Feed My sheep. Truly, I tell you, when you were younger, you dressed yourself and went where you wanted. But when you are old, you will stretch out your hands, and someone else will dress you and lead you where you do not want to go." Jesus said this to indicate the kind of death by which Peter would glorify God. Then He said to Peter, "Follow Me."

Peter turned and saw the disciple whom Jesus loved following them—the one who had leaned against Jesus during the Last Supper and asked, "Lord, who is going to betray You?" Seeing him, Peter asked Jesus, "Lord, what about him?"

Jesus answered, "If I want him to remain alive until I return, what is that to you? You must follow Me."

Because of this, a rumor spread among the believers that this disciple would not die. But Jesus didn't say that; He only said, "If I want him to remain alive until I return, what is that to you?"

This is the disciple who testifies to these things and wrote them down. We know that his testimony is true.

Jesus did many other things as well. If every one of them were written down, I suppose that even the whole world wouldn't have room for the books that would be written.

Amen.

DO YOU BELIEVE GOD?

T hank you for reading *Believe God.*

After reading the personal testimony of an eyewitness to the life of Jesus, has your perspective changed?

Do you see the difference between the Christian religion and the Christian faith—a faith that believes, hopes, and perseveres in the truth about God?

Would you agree that religion and hypocrisy have done more to discredit the Christian faith than even the most vocal and educated skeptics of the Bible?

Did God create man, or did man create God?

When you consider the existence of God from the perspective of truth rather than through the lens of religion, does it help you understand who God may be and what it means to be a child of God?

Jesus is the Son of God, and in Christ, we, too, are called children of God. Can you see why Jesus came into the world to reveal the true nature of God?

Do you believe God is calling you into a relationship with Himself?

No matter how you answer these questions, they remain a deeply personal matter between you and God. You can choose to continue seeking the truth of God, or you can reject Him and accept that this world and this life are all there is.

Perhaps Buddhism, Islam, Hinduism, or one of the many other "isms" out there contain some elements of truth—but are they *true*?

John tells us that Jesus is *The Way, The Truth, and The Life,* and that no one comes to the Father except through Him. If something is truly *true*, it will always lead us to God and to life. If we are people who love and seek truth, that pursuit will always lead us to God—and it will always breathe life into our souls.

Go back and study the Gospel of John more deeply. Get a notebook or journal and write down your thoughts about what John is saying. If the Bible is God's letter to us, then your journal is your letter back to Him. You may be amazed at what you discover in this two-way dialogue with God. This practice transforms prayer from a religious routine into a genuine conversation between a Father and His child.

EPILOGUE

To discover more books of the Bible in the BELIEVE GOD paraphrase version, go to www.believegod.net. This website is a work in progress so keep checking back to discover what is available.

If you are interested in digging deeper into what the Bible is and what we can learn about God, a study Bible is an excellent tool to gain firsthand experience on the nature of God and people. A study Bible is a specialized version of the Bible designed to help readers deepen their understanding of this unique book. It combines the traditional text of the Bible with supplementary resources like commentary, historical and cultural context, tools to dig deeper on topics or words, and practical application tools. Study bibles are tailored for readers ranging from beginners seeking foundational knowledge to seasoned scholars pursuing in-depth study.

Key Features of a Study Bible:

1. Cross-References: Links to related verses elsewhere in Scripture, demonstrating the interconnectedness of biblical texts.

2. Annotations and Commentary: Explanations and notes provided at the bottom or alongside the main text, offering insights into difficult passages, language nuances, and cultural significance.

3. Introductions to Books: Each book of the Bible begins with an introduction that outlines its authorship, historical background, major themes, and purpose.

4. Maps and Timelines: Visual aids that help place events geographically and historically.

5. Concordances: A word index for locating specific terms or concepts within the Bible.

6. Thematic Studies: Sections that explore specific topics, such as faith, grace, or prophecy, across various books.

7. Study Tools: Charts, diagrams, and articles on theology, church history, or biblical languages.

8. Devotional Insights: Reflections that apply biblical teachings to everyday life.

How to Use a Study Bible:

1. Start with Prayer: Begin your study time by asking God for wisdom and understanding. Take several deep breaths and clear your mind and relax and ground your body to open your heart to hear what God has to say to you.

2. Read the Scripture: Focus on the biblical text first to understand its plain meaning. Avoid jumping immediately to the notes or commentary.

3. Use the Commentary: Refer to the notes for explanations of difficult passages or for background on customs, culture, or language. For example, if a verse references a first-century tradition, the commentary can provide clarity.

4. Explore Cross-References: Use the cross-reference system to find related passages. This helps to see how Scripture interprets and supports itself.

5. Examine the Book Introductions: Before diving into a new book, read its introduction to understand the author's purpose, the audience, and the context.

6. Dive into Thematic Studies: Use the thematic or topical studies to explore subjects of interest in a deeper and broader biblical context.

7. Engage with Visual Aids: Review maps and timelines to place events and figures in their proper histor-

ical and geographical setting.

8. Apply What You Learn: Reflect on how the teachings apply to your life. Use the devotional insights or study questions to guide practical application.

9. Keep a Journal: If the Bible is God writing to you, write back. Record your thoughts, questions, and insights in a separate notebook so it is a two-way conversation.

10. Pace Yourself: Avoid the temptation to rush through a book or topic. Allow yourself time to reflect and absorb what the Bible says and experience the reality of a relationship with God.

Tips for Maximizing Your Study Bible:

• Choose a study Bible that aligns with your preferred translation (e.g., NIV, ESV, NKJV). Explore the different translations online to discover which translation appeals to you the most.

• Set a regular time for study to create a consistent habit.

• Combine your study with external resources, like Bible dictionaries or commentaries, for a broader perspective.

• Share your insights and experience with others. Ask questions and share discoveries with friends and family—it is a tremendous way to grow in knowledge, wisdom, and faith.

A study Bible is a powerful tool to enrich your spiritual journey, offering guidance to understand the timeless truths and applying them to your life with clarity and confidence.

www.ingramcontent.com/pod-product-compliance
Lightning Source LLC
Chambersburg PA
CBHW021119130626
46554CB00002B/769